ADR Training

Negotiation and Dispute Resolution Workbook

ADR Training

Negotiation and Dispute Resolution Workbook

Kevin Marshall

Alexys Santos

NITA®

National Institute For Trial Advocacy

Address inquiries to:
Reprint Permission
National Institute for Trial Advocacy
325 W. South Boulder Rd., Ste. 1
Louisville, CO 80027–1130
Phone: (800) 225-6482
Email: permissions@nita.org

Wolters Kluwer

Official co-publisher of NITA.
WKLegaledu.com/NITA

ISBN 978-1-60156-976-9
FBA 1976
eISBN 978-1-60156-977-6
eFBA 1977

Printed in the United States.

Library of Congress Cataloging-in-Publication Data

Names: Marshall, Kevin (Lawyer), author. | Santos, Alexys, author. | National Institute for Trial Advocacy (U.S.), publisher.
Title: ADR training : negotiation and dispute resolution workbook / Kevin Marshall, Alexys Santos.
Description: Louisville, CO : NITA, National Institute for Trial Advocacy, [2022]
Identifiers: LCCN 2022029546 (print) | LCCN 2022029547 (ebook) | ISBN 9781601569769 (trade paperback) | ISBN 9781601569776 (ebook)
Subjects: LCSH: Dispute resolution (Law) | LCGFT: Problems and exercises.
Classification: LCC K2390 .M373 2022 (print) | LCC K2390 (ebook) | DDC 347.09–dc23/eng/20220920
LC record available at https://lccn.loc.gov/2022029546
LC ebook record available at https://lccn.loc.gov/2022029547

SUSTAINABLE FORESTRY INITIATIVE
Certified Chain of Custody
Promoting Sustainable Forestry
www.sfiprogram.org

Table of Contents

Acknowledgments

Our special thanks to Damien Cote for providing valuable contributions to the creation of the teaching notes. Thank you, Todd Berger, for your guidance and encouragement. And finally, thank you to our families for their continued love and support.

FOREWORD

This book contains case problems written by experienced ADR competitors and coaches. Use this resource for holding internal competitions and team training.

As competitors, coaches, and competition organizers, we at Cascadia* recognize team practice as an excellent method for honing a particular skill. For this book, we identified three crucial elements of a successful mediation/negotiation session. The problems in this book are categorized under the skill challenged most predominantly. Make no mistake—each problem in this book requires a team to exercise all these skills. The categorization provides focus for coaches as they select problems for training purposes.

The three categories in this book are:

- problems that foster creative solutions and collaboration with the opposing team,
- problems that require a high level of detail-oriented preparation, and
- problems that encourage teamwork.

Problems indicated with an asterisk (*) are particularly dynamic, and require teams to exhibit collaboration, preparation, and teamwork.

The problems are designed as a hands-on approach to practicing ADR skills. This means that participants should read only the information assigned to their client: Requesting Party *or* Responding Party. Blank pages separate these scenarios to decrease the chances of participants inadvertently reading "spoilers." While only your own integrity prevents you from reading the information for the other party, you will benefit most from these exercises if you avoid reviewing that information.

These problems are designed for a client and counsel but may be modified to counsel and counsel. They can be conducted with a mediator or proceed in a more negotiation-oriented style without a mediator. Teams should both receive the general information, and each team should be assigned either requesting or responding party, respectively.

---

* We are pleased to offer a range of Alternative Dispute Resolution resources. From writing customized problem questions, coaching services, acting as the opposition to your training team, or consulting, please send an email to info@cascadiaadr.com for more information.

CHAPTER ONE

COLLABORATION

Collaboration can be a difficult skill to master in competition. Participating in external competitions offers unparalleled opportunities to engage in mediation/negotiation with teams from around the world. Differences in communication across cultures—such as importance of time, sociocultural norms, religious norms, and others—produce different "styles" of collaboration. Some teams are very cut and dry, leaving little room for discussion beyond the material facts. Others are extremely guarded, revealing minimal information, avoiding questions, and refusing even the most reasonable of offers. We've even seen negotiators who were surprisingly open, providing all their interests upfront before a solid agenda was set. Anticipating how the opposition will engage during the course of a session is a challenge. Coaches can help their teams prepare to face a variety of information sharing and collaboration tactics. Opportunities for achieving collaboration arise not only in matters of information management, but also manifest in behaviors at the mediation/negotiation table. Below are some aspects of collaboration for your consideration.

1.1 Bidirectional Information Gathering

The early stages of a round present numerous unknowns. Seeking first to understand—as a behavior—can reveal a genuine desire on the part of a team to reach a solution on a given issue. It can also build trust at the table, and thereby encourage effective collaboration. Similarly, answering questions directly and substantively also contributes to collaboration and trust-building.

Active listening fosters collaborative conditions as well. Paraphrasing the other party's statements is the low-hanging fruit here; more sophisticated teams will interweave into their discourse clear elements they've heard from the opposite side. Even more impressive teams will reintroduce, later in a round, what they've heard from the other side much earlier (this is not done simply for show—in most cases it's actually a necessary condition to finding a solution). Moreover, at the time of the "sales pitch," effective teams will first frame their offer with the other side's interest highlighted, followed by their own. A full quiver of effective listening skills contributes to collaboration at the table.

1.2 Effective Collaboration During the Brainstorming Phase

When presented with an offer, our first reaction tends to be evaluative. During brainstorming, however, the most effective collaboration happens when both parties air all ideas—before beginning the evaluation process. Show "evaluative restraint" to encourage effective collaboration—the best ideas often grow from a notion that arrives from "out of left field," so welcome those ideas as starting places for crafting a solution, rather than dismissing them out of hand or discouraging exploration by immediately pointing out their downside. Creating a "safe space" in the early stages of a brainstorm enables optimal sharing; only once ideas are exhausted begin systematically evaluating to ascertain the optimal solution while regarding the interests of both parties.

Once all ideas from a brainstorm have surfaced, your team's approach to evaluation will also manifest collaborative behavior—or the lack thereof. For example, seeking first to understand an offer manifests a sincere, constructive, approach. Building on the other side's offer to align it more with your own interests is also collaborative. By contrast, rejecting an offer outright or otherwise evaluating it too prematurely suggests a lack of attempted collaboration—even in those instances where an offer runs contrary to your interests. Even in such a case, you can avoid abandoning collaboration through skills of diplomacy and language to "soften the blow."

1.3 The Role of Emotions and Empathy in the Context of Collaboration

Some fact patterns include tense emotional circumstances between parties—a multi-million-dollar dispute may turn entirely on one party apologizing. Effective collaboration in such cases requires empathy and interpersonal skills, often further complicated by intercultural or intergenerational complexities. Unless a party effectively deals with their emotional issue, it's difficult to achieve collaboration on any other aspects of the dispute.

When faced with an impasse at the table, parties have a variety of options at their disposal—some more aggressive than others. If collaboration is desired, exercise sound judgment. There is a significant difference, for example, in "collaborative signaling" by a party that chooses to use the mediator to overcome an impasse versus a party that chooses to "wave their stick" openly. These are tactical choices informed by empathy (i.e., "reading the room") and not strictly related to information management. They can, however, significantly impact the collaborative dynamic at a table.

For these reasons, the problems in this chapter make excellent choices for final rounds of internal competition. A team that excels in this skill will often perform well in an external competition setting. For this style of case problem, it is imperative that teams prepare creative solutions to each of these problems to present to the opposing side.

The way collaborative opportunities arise in these sessions will vary. Emphasize brainstorming all possible disclosures from the opposing side's confidential information so that teams can prepare their response. It is unwise, however, not to expect to be taken by surprise from time to time. Therefore, choose one of these problems when you want to test a team's ability to think on their feet. If you are preparing opposition against your training team, encourage them to make a major confidential reveal after the training team has used their caucus.

Chapter One Problems

Eye in the Sky

General Information

Drone technology is increasingly used in state defense, policing, and intelligence. Coupled with the widespread availability of high-resolution cameras, anyone owning a drone and a camera can gain visual access to places previously unreachable. While this has vastly enhanced creative photography and videography, drones bring a variety of privacy issues to the forefront of public discourse.

In the case of neighboring nations Kragislovia and Gordingstan, two drastically different perspectives are held on the use of drone technology. Kragislovia is famously liberal and pro-technology. The country has licensed open company and private drone use within its borders. Conversely, neighbor and long-time political ally Gordingstan is skeptical of new technology. The country's populace is more conservative in nature and places a great deal of emphasis on their citizens' right to privacy. Gordingstan has approved drones for military and state defense use only, while private citizen or company use is strictly prohibited. Despite the above-noted differences, the two countries enjoy an amicable history as political and economic allies. The neighboring countries collaborate on everything from border defense to foreign policy and have both benefitted from the alliance. Notably, the countries developed what they call the Kragislovia Gordingstan Select Special Forces Joint Task Force ("KGS Joint Task Force"). This is a joint military force comprised of members of both nations that conducts missions to protect the mutual defense interests of both countries.

Unfortunately, the political alliance faced some difficulty last month when the countries' differing perspectives on drone use came to the forefront of public discussion. Exactly one month ago, an anonymous Kragislovian citizen piloted their drone, mounted with a high-resolution video camera, as it recorded video of the scenic mountainous border region. The video they took was anonymously published to a popular video uploading platform. Within a few hours of its posting, viewers commented that the video captured images just over the border in Gordingstan of a couple out on a hike sharing a kiss. Zooming in on the footage, it became clear that the couple captured on film was none other than famed Gordingstan military man General Marimov and his mistress. The drone footage played on news stations in Kragislovia and Gordingstan alike. The footage embarrassed a well-known general and sparked tension between the nations. The Gordingstan government insisted that drone filming in their country was criminal and demanded that Kragislovia reveal the identity of the drone pilot so they could charge the individual for breach of their privacy laws. Kragislovian officials denied Gordingstan's demands, claiming that the drone flew only over Kragislovian airspace, and did not violate Gordingstan law. Kragislovia further refused to reveal the identity of the drone pilot, stating that the demand was an overreach by Gordingstan considering their citizen was well within their rights to be flying a drone within Kragislovia. Disillusioned, last week the Gordingstan military called a halt to the KGS Joint Task

Force, stating that Gordingstan could no longer trust Kragislovia to have its country's best interests at heart. Political commentators in both countries fear that halting the task force could be the first step in the disintegrating of what was previously a mutually beneficial national alliance.

Sensing that this issue had escalated too far, the Kragislovia government requested mediation with the Gordingstan government. Gordingstan officials agreed. Kragislovia and Gordingstan will both be represented by their respective Ministers of Defense and trusted members of their government legal counsel.

Eye in the Sky
Requesting Party Information

Requesting Party: Kragislovia

The Gordingstan officials' demands offended the Kragislovian government, which feels such requests are insulting to the partnership. Further, Kragislovia believes whole-heartedly in its open approach to drone ownership. This open approach and the resultant developments in drone technology have gained Kragislovia exclusive patents to the world's highest-caliber drones.

According to the Kragislovian intelligence team, the drone footage in question was taken right around the border of Kragislovia and Gordingstan. Your intelligence team worries that the individual's drone might have flown into Gordingstan's air space at a point during the flight. As the Gordingstan military sees any unwanted infringement into Gordingstan air space as an act of war, your government hopes this was not the case. The Kragislovia intelligence team further confirmed that the drone video was taken by a low-level government official, Boris Larislov. Boris publicly opposes Gordingstan's foreign military interventionalist attitude and has been an outspoken critic of General Marimov and his heavy-handed tactics. It is possible that Boris published the video he took intending to harm the Gordingstan military (though Boris has denied this) and your intelligence team fears that if Gordingstan discovers this, the relationship between Kragislovia and Gordingstan will deteriorate further. Without denying any truths, you must avoid compromising Boris's identity or risk causing even more harm to the country's alliance. Fortunately, Boris uploaded the video using identity-protection software. Despite how quickly your intelligence team discovered Boris as the drone pilot, you can rely on this fact to protect your interests during this mediation.

Gordingstan pulling out of the KGS Joint Task Force could have disastrous consequences for Kragislovia. Kragislovia has a weak military presence and losing Gordingstan's protection by way of the task force could invite terrorist bands in the hostile region to invade Kragislovia's borders. Particularly concerning is the presence of terrorist organization Reaper's Soldiers (RS) in the region. RS is known for kidnapping wealthy, high-profile individuals and holding them for ransom. They have done so numerous times in neighboring countries. Surveillance via Kragislovia's high-tech drones has confirmed that the group is growing in numbers. Your government believes that the only thing keeping RS terrorists out of Kragislovia is their fear of retaliation from the Gordingstan military. Kragislovia's immense technological and espionage capacities leave them uniquely positioned to contribute as a partner in the KGS Joint Task Force. You must make it clear that Kragislovia and Gordingstan serve each other better as allies in this unstable region.

Eye in the Sky
Responding Party Information

Responding Party: Gordingstan

While the drone footage of General Marimov and his mistress embarrassed the general, Gordingstan at large was mostly unimpacted. However, the precedent is concerning. The Gordingstanian people value their privacy immensely, and your government will not stand for Kragislovian civilians, companies, or governments capturing footage of any of your citizens without their consent.

To the best of your national intelligence team's knowledge, the drone flight in question did not infringe upon any Gordingstan air space. This is a good thing as any unwanted infringement into Gordingstan air space is seen as an act of war. That said, the wide-angle camera used to capture the drone footage makes it highly probable that drone footage taken on the Kragislovia side of the border will span out to capture video on the Gordingstan side of the border. Video in the high mountains might be harmless, but several Gordingstan villages are within sight of the Kragislovian border. This is a loophole the government never considered when they initially made their anti-drone laws. Today's negotiation must seek to close that loophole and make taking any video footage via drone of Gordingstan lands illegal, regardless of what air space the drone is flying through. Gordingstan has a strong military but their technological capacity lags. In contrast, Kragislovia has a weak military but a world-renowned technology sector. Kragislovia's liberal drone laws have earned them patents to the world's best-known drone technology.

Gordingstan is an immense military power in comparison to Kragislovia; by pulling out of the KGS Joint Task Force, Gordingstan shows Kragislovia just how much they had been relying on Gordingstan's military might for protection. Gordingstan supplies most of the people and resources involved in the task force, and Kragislovia benefits from Gordingstan's protection. Your country is tired of carrying the extra weight in the task force. You must acknowledge, at least among yourselves, that Kragislovia's very favorable trade deals and open access to their thriving economy have helped Gordingstan immensely. Political commentators worry that if Kragislovia responds to the disillusion of the task force by imposing economic sanctions, the already-struggling Gordingstan economy will be pushed to a breaking point. Gordingstan citizens are indifferent on their involvement in the KGS Joint Task Force. However, the military has recently become more aware of the vast capacity drones could have in modern warfare and surveillance. Access to Kragislovia's drone patents would make your strong military immensely more capable. Gordingstan is completely willing to restore the task force and will jump at the chance to do so if Kragislovia grants unlimited and unrestricted access to their drone patents as well as revealing the identity of the individual who piloted the drone so Gordingstan intelligence can investigate further.

PUNCHER'S CHANCE*

General Information

Castel "the Cannon" Carlito, is a well-known professional boxer. A respected competitor, Castel is known for putting on a show while getting into brawling fights—and often coming out on top—against the best boxing talent from around the world. Castel has worked to become a top tier pro and has been competing professionally for the last nine years.

The promoter, Pat Baron, is infamous in the boxing sphere for their eccentric personality and stable of high-level competitors. Baron's promotion company, Crown Sport Promotion (CSP), represents much of boxing's top talent. CSP has represented Castel for the past four years. Under their contract, an exclusivity clause ensures that Castel is promoted only by CSP for the next six years of their career (ten years total). This arrangement is mutually beneficial, as CSP retains a portion of all the profits from Castel's pay-per-view fights.

Boxing is a young person's game, and a savvy fighter like Castel knows their career could be cut short at any time. Castel is always trying to make as much money per fight as they can while in their prime. As such, Castel approached Baron, seeking permission to be temporarily released from the exclusivity clause to accept a potentially lucrative exhibition fight under another promotion company against a well-known internet personality. In exchange, Castel would give CSP a portion of their earnings for the bout. Baron seemed receptive to the idea at first. This would provide CSP the opportunity to earn a significant amount of money without any promotional work (which can be quite expensive). During their initial closed-door meeting, Baron verbally agreed to the deal with Castel and their agent. Sometime after this agreement, however, Baron called Castel and reneged their agreement, citing that releasing Castel from the conditions of their contract, no matter how brief, was too risky. Castel was furious. Immediately after the initial meeting when Baron gave their consent, Castel's agent had called and accepted the exhibition fight. Castel advised Baron that if they did not honor their agreement, Castel would retire and leave CSP without one of their best fighters. This did not go over well with Baron.

Within a few hours, Castel received a formal letter from CSP demanding repayment of a loan issued to Castel four years ago when they first signed with CSP. The loan was for $150,000 and was subject to a repayment period of ten years interest free, or within forty-eight hours of whenever CSP demanded repayment. Castel's contract stipulates that without timely repayment CSP retains the right to claim Castel's assets as collateral for the loan. CSP could conceivably take Castel's car and family home if the forty-eight-hour window expires.

Upon receiving the demand-for-repayment notice, Castel contacted Baron to request an immediate mediation/negotiation to settle the pressing issues at hand.

Baron agreed to a meeting in CSP's office boardroom the next day. Castel, Baron (on behalf of CSP promotion), and their respective councils meet at the mediation table with twenty-four hours remaining on the demanded loan repayment. At the table the parties will need to discuss 1) loan repayment, 2) the proposed exhibition, 3) their business relationship moving forward, and 4) the remainder of Castel's boxing career.

Puncher's Chance
Requesting Party Information

Requesting Party: Castel

For Castel this has escalated too quickly for comfort. Castel accepted the loan from CSP when they needed financial support to purchase their family home. At the time of signing, they were verbally reassured that the forty-eight-hour reclaim clause was just a standard precaution and would never be enforced against them in practice. At the time, Castel was extremely grateful for the loan. Castel has sufficient funds to repay the $150,000, but this is spread across numerous investments and other ventures. Liquidating these funds would take at least two weeks, which is well outside of the CSP's demand. The prospect of their spouse and children losing their family home is devastating to Castel. Castel is willing to do what they can to ensure this does not happen. If an agreement cannot be reached on the outstanding issues between the parties, they will at least seek permission to repay the loan in full in fourteen days. This is essential for Castel during the course of this mediation/negotiation.

It is a well-known "secret" that CSP has a history of exploitive contracts with fighters. Despite this, Castel never expected this would happen to them. When they decided to sign with CSP five years into their career, they were not making as much money as they felt they deserved. CSP has a reputation of promoting the world's top fighters and earning them significant wealth and fame. While Castel has earned only marginally more money fighting under CSP, their popularity has grown tenfold. While CSP's promotion may have played a role, at this point in their career, Castel believes they would have been making more under another promoter. Moreover, CSP's immediate action of this forty-eight-hour clause makes Castel highly suspicious of what other hidden clauses may exist in the contract signed four years ago. Castel is uncomfortable continuing to fight under the current contract as it stands. If they are to continue to fight under CSP, they prefer that a new agreement be drafted between the parties.

The proposed exhibition match was an incredible opportunity for Castel. Despite their accrued fame and skill, Castel has yet to earn a seven-figure payday, something that is commonplace for boxers of this esteem. This exhibition fight was the first opportunity to do so. Castel is getting older and is aware that their time as a top-level competitor is finite. Barring any serious injuries, Castel would likely be able to fight another three years but would like to retire within two. Before this exhibition fight was offered, Castel was already contemplating the prospect of early retirement. Now it seems they are confronted with the possibility and must decide what the rest of their career will look like. This fight is a once-in-a-career opportunity for Castel, and Baron reneging their initial acquiescence is incredibly disheartening.

Castel's lawyer advised them that a verbal agreement in the presence of a witness (Castel's agent, Hector Hughes) gives rise to a legitimate argument that the contract had been temporarily dissolved in the eyes of the law. However, it would still be up for a judge to decide based on the facts. If Castel accepts the fight despite CSP's refusal, and CSP pursues litigation and wins, Castel stands to lose most of the potential earnings. Therefore, it would be more beneficial to receive CSP's explicit written permission to undertake the fight. Knowing that money is Baron's ultimate motivator, Castel is willing to offer CSP a maximum of 30 percent of the earnings from this bout. Offering CSP a higher percentage than this would cut too far into Castel' earnings and make retiring after the fight an impossibility. Castel needs to do whatever they can to make this exhibition happen; they will have to alleviate any concerns CSP has in order to do so.

One of Castel's bargaining tools is their fame in their tiny home country of East Andrui, a country known as a hotbed of young boxing talent. Castel is a hero to many of these young fighters and is constantly on East Andrui news and sports television. An interview or press release that paints CSP in a negative light is likely to ensure no top tier talent from the country signs with CSP, while conversely, a positive interview or press release is likely to seriously increase the chances of CSP signing more East Andruian talent for years to come. CSP's poor dealings with Castel have triggered some moral reservations about Castel issuing a positive endorsement of CSP, but if Castel feels they have been treated with enough respect and fairness at this upcoming mediation/negotiation they are open to doing so.

Puncher's Chance
Responding Party Information

Responding Party: Pat Baron (on behalf of CSP)

Castel is a fan favorite fighter who would appeal to many other promoters. They have been a nest egg for CSP for the last two years or so and their stock is only rising. Despite being under contract for an additional six years, effectively the rest of Castel's career, any boxer can elect to retire from the sport at any time. If Castel *does* retire and fights again within the next six years, they will have to do so under CSP promotion. Though Castel has complete autonomy in deciding when to retire, it would be terrible if they followed through on the threat. CSP stands to make significant money off Castel's fights moving forward. The name alone is sufficient to earn $200,000 per fight, win or lose. Ideally, Castel fights for the remainder of the six-year contract, but CSP would be happy with a minimum of three more years of fighting from Castel under their promotion. If this could be ensured contractually in the upcoming mediation/negotiation, CSP could be flexible with their other terms.

You don't have much experience with exhibitions and can't imagine they would be very lucrative. When Castel initially approached you with the offer, you liked the idea of profiting from this fight without any expenditure in terms of advertising and promoting. However, now you are worried about the precedent it would set with other fighters under CSP promotion to temporarily dissolve the exclusivity clause in the contract. If you allow this exhibition to move forward, you want 35 percent of Castel's fight earnings in order to make it worthwhile. This requirement will surely prevent other fighters from making similar demands (or, if they do, would provide substantial profit to CSP).

Originally, the plan was to threaten litigation if Castel moved forward with the exhibition fight without repaying the $150,000 loan in its entirety. However, upon receiving legal advice, you are uncertain whether such a contract term is legal. CSP is worried that if Castel has discovered an illegal term, the entire contract will be considered null and void. It may be wise to redraft a fresh contract altogether to avoid addressing the legality of the current contract. However, you are worried that Castel's lawyer will attempt to strongarm you into an agreement that allows Castel to fight the exhibition while providing few of the proceeds. Your lawyer suspects that Castel will rely on the verbal agreement between yourself and Castel and their agent to contend that this has legitimate legal basis. Luckily, your sources have informed you that Castel's agent, Hector Hughes, is running an illegal underground fighting ring which would bring him severe legal and financial penalties, including jail time. This would likely make him lose all credibility in court. Although you don't want to fight dirty during this negotiation, you will threaten to expose Hector should Castel prove difficult. You must strike a balance between your demands and keeping Castel on CSP's team.

Castel is one of the most famous celebrities in their tiny home country of East Andrui. CSP recognized years ago that East Andrui had plenty of high-level boxing talent. Despite many trips to the country, you have been unsuccessful in recruiting any notable talent from East Andrui with the exception of Castel. CSP would stand to make a lot of money if they could use Castel's influence to represent top East Andruian talent.

TRIBAL TURBULENCE*

General Information

The year is 3067. Nuclear war in 2589 laid waste to the world as it was known. The few survivors (known as the new pioneers) struggled to extract resources out of the barren wasteland that was Old Earth. Over time, these four distinct tribes formed on New Earth:

1) *The Firebreathers*
2) *The Willows*
3) *New Atlantis*
4) *The Cascadians*

The four tribes split apart around 2700 to seek out natural resources in different environments. The Firebreathers went to the hottest climates and sought to utilize solar power. The Willows went to the old forests, New Atlantis to the sea, and the Cascadians went to the mountains.

The tribes carved out independent existences, lording over their own relative domains for many years. For three centuries the tribes coexisted peacefully. However, sometime around the year 3000 resources started becoming scarce . . .

New Atlantis's unsustainable overfishing practices have begun to catch up with them. The resulting fish scarcity threatens to completely deplete their primary source of food. New Atlantis has subsisted on meagre portions of fish and coconuts, but they cannot do so much longer. In a desperate attempt to regain resources, New Atlantis sent representatives from their tribe to broker a shared resources arrangement with the Willows. The Willows did not take kindly to visitors infringing on their space and threatened the scouts that if they did not leave immediately, they would hold them prisoner.

The scouts returned to New Atlantis with the bad news. The New Atlantis chief (Chief Poseidon) was furious that the Willows treated guests with such disrespect. Tales spread far and wide across New Earth of the might of the New Atlantis navy after they defeated the Firebreathers some fifty years ago (known colloquially as "The Extinguishing"). The Willows have few military resources and would not fare very well in combat against New Atlantis if tensions escalated. In one desperate final attempt at diplomacy, Chief Poseidon is traveling to the forest of the Willows with trusted council to broker a deal to obtain access to food for the people of New Atlantis. If this attempt at diplomacy is unsuccessful, Chief Poseidon will have no choice but to make the long and dangerous boat journey to the Cascades to seek the help of the mountain people.

Since The Extinguishing, New Atlantis has no contact with the Firebreathers. The battle ended with the Firebreathers escaping by the skin of their teeth and fleeing the shoreline and water under New Atlantis rule. Making a peace deal for resources with the contentious Firebreather tribe seemed improbable before The Extinguishing; after the battle, it seems an impossibility.

In contrast, New Atlantis and the Cascadians have had a friendly tribal partnership for years and all previous contact with the tribe has been pleasant. However, the Cascadians are geographically very difficult to reach. Boats often capsize in the rough coastal waters. Moreover, the long journey by boat makes taking food supplies back from the Cascadians to New Atlantis very difficult.

Chief Poseidon arrived at the forest of the Willows tribe and was welcomed by their elected leader Elder Redwood. Elder Redwood greeted Chief Poseidon warmly and agreed to the chief's request for a private meeting. Attending the mediation/negotiation will be Chief Poseidon and counsel representing New Atlantis, alongside Elder Redwood and counsel representing the Willows.

Tribal Turbulence
Requesting Party Information

Requesting Party: Chief Poseidon (New Atlantis)

Of course, you are quite offended with the way the Willows rejected your scouts who sought help from their people. Your pride almost prevented you from making this journey, but love for ruling your people has kept you moving forward. New Atlantis must broker peace or risk starvation. Birth rates are high and food supply is consistently declining. The tribe is growing discontent and you have heard mutterings that a coup will form to overthrow you if things do not improve soon. You will do what you can to determine the needs of the Willows, as bartering a deal to secure a source of food is essential to keeping the New Atlantians content and your position as chief secure. In total, you have 650 people to feed: 325 are men, 275 are women, and 50 are children. You must secure enough food to feed as many as possible. You hope that the Willows have sufficient food to spare, as it may be offensive to ask them to deplete their people's food source for your own people. New Atlantis must be respectful and aware of any cultural differences between the tribes at the negotiation/mediation table.

The Firebreathers are sworn enemies of New Atlantis, and the warring tribes have not seen or heard from each other in decades. When your scouts returned, they reported overhearing the Willows's forest guards complaining about the Firebreathers and the destruction they have caused. You became immediately suspicious upon hearing this report. Conspicuous and destructive behavior is often a symptom of growing power. You suspect that the Firebreathers may be organizing an attack upon New Atlantis, not suspecting that New Atlantis would ever communicate with the Willows. An attack on your starving people would devastate New Atlantis: it might eradicate your people forever. You must gather as much information as you can from Elder Redwood to determine the Firebreather's location and intentions and possibly prepare your people for battle. If your suspicions are correct, this makes your desperation to secure a food source even stronger. Though your army is large, an attack during this period of instability would surely destroy everything the New Atlantians have worked for.

A possible leverage point is New Atlantis's strong relationship with the Cascadians. New Atlantis ventured by boat to Cascadia many years ago and made peace with the Cascadians. The tribal leaders agreed that they would help each other in the future by any means possible. Cascadians enjoy plentiful resources, especially meat, hides, and tools carved from stone. You are confident that if you could only bridge the distance between yourselves and the Cascadians, there would never be another worry about New Atlantis's food shortages. Perhaps the Willows would be interested in helping you bridge this gap, and you will come up with a few ideas for doing so before the meeting. This would be mutually beneficial to you and the Willows.

For years, New Atlantis's tribe shaman spoke of a long-lost tribe that ventured to Mars before the nuclear war. Known colloquially as "the Red Raiders," they were apparently a highly intelligent and benevolent people who had offered to assist anyone who was willing to escape to Mars. The few who trusted the Red Raiders, who declared that the end of the world as it was known was ending, are rumored to be living extraordinarily well on the Red Planet. If those on Earth could reach and sustain a height of 1,000 yards into the atmosphere, they could potentially signal to the lost tribe and begin a dialogue. This would likely take substantial time and resources, so a thorough plan must be formulated to do so.

Tribal Turbulence
Responding Party Information

Responding Party: Elder Redwood (The Willows)

The Willows deeply regret threatening the scouts who came on behalf of New Atlantis. The Willows have been constantly tormented by bands of renegade Firebreathers. These factions of the Firebreathers are nomadic and set up camp at the edge of the forest, stealing food supplies and technology, and harming the native tribespeople. They have been getting creative lately in their deception and the Willows's forest patrol guard believed that the New Atlantis scouts sent by Chief Poseidon were renegade Firebreathers in disguise. The Willows need to find a way to deal with the troublesome Firebreathers, as their constant thievery is a threat to the food supply and safety of their people. When the guards discovered the true identity of the scouts, they attempted to contact the scouts and apologize for how they treated them (the Willow people are normally immensely hospitable). However, they were unable to reach them in time. Elder Redwood hopes to clear this issue up at the mediation/negotiation.

The tribe must broker peace, not just with New Atlantis but amongst the tribes at large. They know that even with their guerrilla warfare tactics they are no match for the naval might of New Atlantis. Chief Poseidon and the people of New Atlantis are proud, and Elder Redwood and council must be respectful and aware of any cultural differences between the tribes. Ultimately, the Willows tribe respects New Atlantis for their integrity and warrior spirit that reminds them of the pioneers of New Earth.

The Willows have a relatively stable source of food through forest wildlife and growth. Elder Redwood appreciates New Atlantis having the decency to barter a deal for a food source instead of poaching like the Firebreathers. The Willows have enough for themselves with some to spare for the people of New Atlantis, provided they can cut down or eliminate the Firebreathers' thievery and extortion. You are unsure of the number of New Atlantians, but you have enough spare food for 550 people provided that 300 or fewer are men.

The Willows, the most technologically advanced of the four tribes, have recently developed a new ground-breaking travel technology called "Flutter-Spokes." Modeled on the airplanes of Old Earth, Flutter-Spokes harness the power of the wind through built-in turbines and the power of the sun through solar panels to create a self-sufficient flying machine that can reach heights of over 3,000 feet for sustained periods of time. This would allow safer travel in less than a quarter of the time typical boat travel takes. The Willows are willing to disclose their innovative technology provided they have a stable partner in New Atlantis and that disclosing this information benefits them. You would like a promise of protection from the Firebreathers and other rogue warriors for years to come.

The Willows tribe desires peace with the Cascadians, who they know to be a good, moral people. While Flutter-Spokes have the potential to take the Willow's tribe to Cascadia on a peace mission, this has yet to happen. The Willows lack military strength and worry that if they come to the Cascadians with their hand out that they will be taken over by military might. The tribe should seek a solution to this at today's mediation/negotiation.

Trouble in Paradise*

* This problem was used in the preliminary round of the Transatlantic Negotiation Competition.

General Information

World renowned master-chef Sam Ferrari and exclusive food and wine supplier "Complete Foods" (CF) have enjoyed an outstanding working relationship over the past ten years.

Sam is the sole owner and head chef of the highly regarded fine-dining restaurant "Bellissimo." Both Bellissimo and CF are located on the tropical island country of "Aral." Aral is known for its beautiful beaches, rolling surf, and friendly locals. More recently, it has been a popular vacation destination for self-described "foodies" from around the world. Bellissimo is the only three-star Michelin restaurant on the island and CF is currently the only major quality food provider. For a decade Bellissimo and CF have enjoyed an exclusive contract, governed under Aral law. The contract stipulates:

1) *CF will be the sole provider of food and wine products for Bellissimo's island restaurant.*
2) *CF is responsible for ensuring the quality of its products.*
3) *Bellissimo will receive an exclusive 15 percent discount off regular-priced food.*
4) *Bellissimo will receive an exclusive 25 percent discount off regular-priced wine.*

The existing contract is subject to being dissolved and renegotiated if any of the four conditions fail to be satisfied by either party.

Crisis came six months ago when Crown Prince Aman of the country Dabi and esteemed French food critic Ester Lupin were dining at Bellissimo. The pair was quietly enjoying the ambience of Bellissimo and relaxing into the laid-back island lifestyle until wine was served with dinner. After their first sip of wine, Prince Aman immediately became sick, while Ester spat out her wine. The wine was spoiled and unsuitable to drink. Storming out of the restaurant, Ester assured Sam and anyone else in the restaurant who would listen that she would be telling the world just how horrible her experience at Bellissimo was. Prince Aman left silently, directly to his private jet to leave his island vacation early and return to Dabi.

Sam was furious with CF. Ester was an influential food critic and Prince Aman a trendsetter with notable sway over the affluent population of Dabi. Sam's restaurant stood to take serious economic and reputational loss because of the spoiled wine.

After multiple angry telephone calls back and forth between Sam and the CEO of CF, the previously amicable business relationship was dissolving. Sam's lawyer emailed the CF CEO last month with the following requests:

A) Dissolve the current contract due to breach of contract under condition 2.

B) Pay for loss of reputation amounting to $3 million.

C) Pay for economic losses over the past six months of $500,000.

The CEO of CF denies blame, stating that all products left its location with no quality concerns. Sam threatens to leave Aral and open a restaurant on the mainland if the parties don't come to a solution soon. Before the recent crisis Sam and CF planned on meeting in the next few months to discuss renewing or amending their current contract, which expires in six months. Complete Foods requested mediation/negotiation to resolve this issue, to which Sam agreed. Both Complete Foods and Sam will be represented by their respective councils, who have both been given full settlement authority.

Trouble in Paradise
Requesting Party Information

Responding Party: Sam Ferrari

You know from your conversations with Sam that Sam can be quite emotional. Sam regrets threatening to leave the island of Aral. They love their new island home and have no desire to take their restaurant elsewhere now that cooler heads have prevailed. Moreover, Sam's initial requests for damages and dissolving the current contract seem heavy-handed. Sam told you in a previous meeting that they discovered a few weeks ago the spoiled wine in question had been opened prematurely by Bellissimo staff. It is likely there was still an error in handling from CF, but the negligent actions of Sam's staff make this harder to ascertain. The terms of the contract are unclear as to who would be at fault for the low-quality product, and your case for dissolving the contract is unlikely to succeed. Sam still believes the issue was unrelated to their team's handling of the wine and is upset with CF for their lack of accountability, especially after years of working together.

In researching economic damages, your legal team discovered that food critic Ester Lupin's influence was not nearly as vast as previously imagined. While Ester's food blogs were immensely popular over the last five years, recent personal and professional scandal has dropped her influence significantly over the past six months. No "real foodies" take Ester's opinions seriously anymore, and your legal team deemed her negative review (published on her blog) unlikely to influence potential Bellissimo customers.

However, Prince Aman referred to his poor experience dining at Bellissimo on a Dabi television interview. This bad press is likely to amount to a 4 percent decrease in tourism from Dabi over the next ten years (which Sam has already noticed) and total future lost profit of around $1–1.5 million over the next ten years for Bellissimo (at which time the interview becomes irrelevant and is unlikely to affect future profit). Sam, who is keen to cover potential losses, wants CF to compensate them at least $1 million for the incident.

The contract stipulates that Sam must negotiate with CF upon the contract expiring. There is no obvious reason to look elsewhere as CF has been a profitable partner over the previous decade. Sam made more money over the past ten years than they ever dreamed possible. Bellissimo operates under a great business model, and despite the recent damage to reputation, stands to continue being profitable. Getting quality foods and wine to the island is challenging and you know of no other companies with the food and wine quality standards of CF. Before this incident, their wine was always top quality and at a price better than any other distributer. Yet, Aral is an emerging destination and is likely to attract more quality food and wine suppliers with continued industry growth. For this reason, Sam would prefer to avoid an exclusive contract that binds him to CF for an extended period; however, Sam doesn't envision a company matching CF's ability to meet Bellissimo's needs any time soon.

Sam has instructed your team that it is crucial to obtain a written apology from CF as a sign of goodwill in their relationship in addition to as much compensation as possible for the incident, without being unreasonable. You also have Sam's permission to negotiate a future contact with CF, which Sam feels could be improved considering how strong of a partner Bellissimo has been. Any future contract should address the four points of the initial agreement.

Trouble in Paradise
Responding Party Information

Requesting Party: Complete Foods

CF was blindsided by the accusations of poor product quality. Never in their fifteen years of business has anyone accused them of providing a low-quality product. Before internally investigating the issue, CF's CEO received multiple insulting and disrespectful voicemails from Sam Ferrari. Sam's lawyer proposed payments outrageously high by anybody's estimation and created more animosity. The reputational damage to Bellissimo will likely amount to half of what Sam has requested or less. Tempers flared and CF's CEO became stubborn, refusing to admit any potential culpability. This falling out is inconsistent with the goodwill and friendship the parties have shared over the past ten years of business.

CF's investigation of the incident discovered that the wine was bottled by a CF employee who was later fired for negligence and a failure to abide by company health and safety standards. That employee has not responded to calls or emails from the company. It is impossible to say for certain, however it seems likely that there could have been an error in product quality consistent with this former employee's poor attention to detail. Sam is unlikely to know this information, as the employee's firing was discreet and handled in-house. Despite a likely error on CF's end, no conclusive proof has surfaced, and as such, it is unlikely that there is cause for dissolving the current contract.

CF provides exceptional ingredients and quality wine. Before Bellissimo came to the island, business was suffering. The locals lacked interest in quality food and wine products. The exclusive supply contract with Sam saved the business and made the last ten years marginally profitable.

The high-quality food and wine market is growing in Aral. CF's CEO has alerted your legal team that rival food manufacturer, IGC (International Grocery Conglomerate), plans to open a branch on the island. It is almost certain that IGC will court Bellissimo and, due to the company's size, offer less expensive food products with the trade-off of slightly worse quality. However, IGC does not sell wine and Sam is unlikely to find quality wine at the price point CF offers from any other suppliers.

Though the last ten years have been profitable for CF, Bellissimo has had immense success and profitability. Sam has amassed a small fortune in revenue from the successful restaurant. CF intended to negotiate for a more beneficial profit split model before the recent crisis or news of incoming competitor IGC. In light of the recent considerations and being mindful of Sam's temper, you have been instructed that it would be sufficient to renew the contract as it stands for another five to ten years to ensure CF keeps Sam's business and as a sign of positivity towards a future business relationship. Any future contract should address the four points of the initial agreement.

CF cannot stand for Bellissimo to leave the island or to lose Sam's business. Your legal team has been instructed to do what they can to mend the relationship without compromising CF's reputation. You have been instructed that you can offer between $500,000 and $1 million as compensation for the crisis, provided Sam renews the current contract for at least another five years.

ARCTIC VIROLOGY*

General Information

Alixena and Celestia are remote countries located near the North Pole. Centuries ago, native people inhabited both countries. But the barren and unforgiving land was ultimately ill-suited to sustain human life. The natives migrated southward over 500 years ago, an act anthropologists have attributed to the need for access to food and medicine.

For the last nine decades, scientists have inhabited Alixena and Celestia, coming north from the southern region to conduct extended periods of research. Mountainous terrain divides Alixena from Celestia and the inhabitants of the two countries have little relationship with one another. Although they are respectively supplied with resources from various southern countries, on occasion one country sends a signal urgently requesting medicine or other supplies and the other country always obliges. This is the extent of the relationship between Alixena and Celestia.

Both Alixena and Celestia are completely encrusted in a thick layer of permafrost. It is settled fact that climate change threatens to devastate the Arctic region. Melting glaciers create instability that greatly impacts the livelihood of species that rely on the glaciers to access food and water. Scientists have been collecting and analyzing soil and glacial samples to monitor the changing climate situation. Sasha Vrai, a renowned virologist studying in Celestia, was conducting a routine analysis when they discovered an ancient virus in a glacial sample. This sample may indicate that disease, rather than food shortages, is what drove the native people to move south.

Although finding ancient viruses in soil samples is not uncommon, such a finding in the Arctic region poses an unusual set of problems. Since the viruses here are suspended in ice, climate change (and thus melting ice and snow) threatens to recirculate these viruses into the air, which could potentially reinfect humans. Sasha initially hoped that such an outbreak could be contained; however, polar winds circulate from the Arctic and blow southward rapidly, meaning that the virus could travel south and infect millions of people without warning and with no vaccine. Concerned, Sasha and their colleagues immediately alerted Alixena to the discovery.

Alixenian scientist Salem Watts traveled to Celestia accompanied by two other virologists and arrived within twenty-four hours. The conversation began civilized, but tempers soon ran high. Salem fiercely demanded that this sample be studied in the Arctic to understand the history of the Alixenian and Celestian natives. They demand that the virus's DNA be sequenced and compared to the human remains to understand the historic epidemiology of the virus that infected them, thus forcing them to move southward. Sasha vehemently rejects this idea, claiming that it is critical to send the sample south so that immunologists and virologists can begin to develop a vaccine if the virus eventually travels south. Salem scoffs at the notion, saying that the odds are too miniscule to raise such concerns.

Nothing was settled that evening. Despite the disagreement, Salem and colleagues were invited to stay the evening in Celestia. The next morning, when everyone had cooled down, Sasha suggested that they set a time to mediate/negotiate the dispute. Both parties agreed and promised they would not alert anyone in the southern region of the discovery until an agreement is reached. Coincidentally, two of the scientists (one from Celestia and one from Alixena) are licensed attorneys and will act as counsel during the discussion.

Arctic Virology
Requesting Party Information

Requesting Party: Sasha Vrai

You are honestly shocked that you and Salem are so far apart on how to handle this situation. Ethics should be at the forefront of all scientific studies, and you were certain that all good scientists would protect human life over all else. Clearly, you erred when your team informed Alixena of the virus. During this discussion, you must keep policy considerations and protection of society at the forefront of all your decisions.

You have yet to show the Alixenian virologists the sample and therefore only have the perspective of your own team. However, early analysis indicates that this virus may be an early mutation Palrexia-33, an intestinal virus that wiped out many early civilizations in the south several hundred years ago. This virus disappeared before the development of vaccines, and therefore modern humans are still susceptible to infection. Your best educated guess is that even with accelerated human trials, it will take over two years to develop a vaccine against Palrexia-33. Therefore, you think sending the sample to your colleagues in the south immediately is imperative, so that they can begin working on research to develop a vaccine. Unfortunately, there is one major obstacle: the sample is not large enough to effectively develop a vaccine. You need a team of field scientists to explore the area that surrounds Celestia and Alixena. In fact, you initially collected the sample on your week off. You had travelled to the mountain ridge that separates Celestia from Alixena on a mountaineering expedition and collected samples along the route. The sample that contained Palrexia-33 was collected more than halfway through your trip and likely was within the Alixenian border. You therefore need express permission from Alixena to start this project.

The promise not to alert anyone in the south to the discovery of Palrexia-33 was too late. As a passionate virologist, you emailed your spouse, also a practicing virologist who is working in the south. Your spouse also lives in a remote location and communication is slow. Your email detailed your findings, and you received a response the morning after the argument with Salem. The response read:

"Amazing news. Send 2 Doris 4 testing. Can't wait 2 hear more."

When you promised Salem that you would not inform anyone about this, your email had slipped your mind. Tempers had already run so high, and you were willing to do anything to resolve this dispute in a pragmatic manner. You sent an email back in the morning, which read:

"Issues here. Pls do not tell anyone about this. Have u already? Talk soon."

Your emails typically take three hours to send. You won't know whether your spouse told anyone else about the virus until after the mediation takes place. Doris Peters, to whom your spouse refers in their email, is a colleague specializing in vaccine development. She works at a massive research centre at Southern University. It is entirely possible that your spouse informed Doris in their excitement about your discovery, but you won't be certain until you receive a response to your last email. If Doris *does* know about Palrexia-33, then she will certainly have informed all her colleagues at Southern University (your alma mater), which also funds your research. Your supervisor will expect you to comply with their wishes which will almost certainly be to find a vaccine. If word about Palrexia-33 spreads to the public, you worry what the public opinion will be. You know that the Alixena camp has much faster modes of communication. You'd like to bring up the possibility of using their internet to contact both your spouse and Doris to be certain. You are worried that Salem may view this as a breach of trust, therefore you must be very careful about when and how you bring this up during the meeting.

You want to draft a contract with Alixena about how to deal with Palrexia-33 to protect your interests (and the interests of society at large). You also anticipate that you will both want to explore at the border between the two countries. This dispute may initiate a professional relationship between the Celestian and Alixenian camps. Undertaking joint scientific projects would result in a lucrative and successful partnership between the two camps. Alixena has superior technology for conducting on-site research. You are uncertain whether their funding is sufficient, but Southern University is liberal in funding projects. You want to suggest combining resources with the Alixenian scientists. Therefore, the key issues you want the contract to resolve are:

A) How this first sample will be handled;

B) The particulars about searching for further samples of Palrexia-33;

C) Who has the final decision-making responsibility for future scientific discoveries along the border of Celestia and Alixena; and

D) The profit split, if any, for use of Palrexia-33.

As far as searching for additional samples of Palrexia-33, you are confident that Southern University will fund this project in full and send a full team of field scientists to help with that endeavour (if it is to develop a vaccine). You simply need permission from Alixena to do so. You also want final decision-making power regarding this first project, and in exchange Alixena will make the final decisions on the next two projects and then alternating for every project after that.

With respect the profit sharing, you are not very particular about the split. You will seek 70 percent of the profits for this first Palrexia-33 project; after all, you discovered it. You feel that whoever has the decision-making power for a particular project thereafter should retain 55 percent of the profits.

You will benefit from partnering with Alixena as well—it is no secret that their technological resources are superior to yours. If this mediation/negotiation succeeds, you are confident it will mark the beginning of a fruitful scientific relationship that will greatly benefit humankind.

Arctic Virology
Responding Party Information

Responding Party: Salem Watts

You are honestly shocked at how Sasha handled this situation. Advancing scientific knowledge should be any respectable scientists' priority. Of course, ethical principles underpin every decision. Your position is that understanding the epidemiology of this disease *is* the most ethical choice. You consulted your colleagues, and they agree that the amount of virus is too small and the distance from the mainland too large to threaten infecting the general population.

Little is understood about the indigenous peoples that inhabited Celestia and Alixena five centuries ago. There is a small community of people in the southeast who trace their ancestry to these civilizations. A common story shared throughout this community is that the Celestians and Alixenians were forced to migrate suddenly and without warning when an illness ran rampant throughout their villages. Though not settled fact, scientists believed that this virus was an early mutation of M4N4, a deadly blood-borne virus which resurged in the population seventy years ago. If Sasha and his colleagues believe this new virus to be M4N4, then the general population has immunity and developing a vaccine would be a waste of resources.

Your promise not to inform anyone in the south of the discovery came too late. When Sasha initially contacted you via radio to inform you of the discovery, you immediately sent an email to your friend and colleague, Henny Thrunston, in your excitement, and shared your theory. Henny lives in the community of indigenous people, and replied:

> "Dearest Salem,
>
> I am delighted to hear of this news. I feel that this is the first discovery that will finally answer so many questions that our people have about our great migration 500 years ago. I have informed a few of our Elders, who want me to communicate that we would be delighted send people to help you in any way we can. I am so excited to finally know whether this discovery will bring us closer to the truth of my people."

Obviously, this is going to be an uncomfortable topic to discuss during this mediation. You did not intend to make any misrepresentations to Sasha, but tempers ran high, and you genuinely forgot about the exchange with Henny until the morning after your discussion. Ultimately, you feel that Henny and their people have a right to know their history, and to deny them this opportunity would be unethical. Therefore, you must insist that this first sample be used to determine whether this virus is a variation of M4N4, and even if it is not, whether it infected the native people of Celestia and Alixena.

You and your colleagues were researching the cause of the "great migration," but had predicted that it was related to animal migration patterns. As such, your team has meticulously plotted the topography of both countries and possess accurate maps of the entire area. With Henny's offer to send people to the Arctic to help, it would be simple to launch a project to obtain more samples of this virus. Also, once word spreads to the public, there will certainly be social movements that call for the empowerment of these indigenous peoples and demands to expedite the process so that their truth can be told. Unfortunately, you spent most your research budget from Southeastern University on the technology used to survey the land and creating maps to understand migratory routes. You require more funding. You know that Sasha and his team would benefit from the excellent technology your camp possesses. You also feel that if you can work together toward a solution, both teams can collaborate on future projects, which would be extremely lucrative for both. If this first project proves successful, you would like to continue researching animal migration since it benefits animal conservation. However, such an undertaking is expensive, and you would benefit from the additional funding from Southern University (which funds Sasha's projects). Luckily, zoologists pay well for conservation data.

You want to propose the following arrangement to Sasha:

A) That you use this initial sample to study the epidemiology of this virus within the context of Alixena and Celestia;

B) That the profits from this first project be used to fund subsequent collaborative projects exclusively;

C) That Salem has final decision-making authority with respect to this first project; and

D) That Sasha and you will share decision-making authority on all subsequent projects, and if a decision cannot be agreed upon, then a neutral third party will make the decision.

If this mediation goes well, it could mark the beginning of a very fruitful scientific relationship between Alixena and Celestia.

Chapter Two

Preparation

Introduction

Inevitably, teams begin their negotiation/mediation with information deficiencies. Preparation requires scenario development and analysis. To achieve this, teams use the facts provided and map out a "logic tree"—an analytical framework to help navigate the expected unknowns. In fact, this becomes the backbone of a team's entire preparation; the framework serves to clearly identify:

1) the questions the team will ask (i.e., given the unknowns);
2) the options to advance during a brainstorm (and the information needed prior to introducing them); and
3) the gradation of each of the team's options and the incremental movement possible across said gradation during the negotiation (ideally linked to predetermined, interest-based thresholds).

An example of this exercise follows this introduction.

Assess facts critically by identifying the incomplete information trails. Use this analysis to prepare questions, spot oddities that warrant further inquiry (which is often an indicator of the existence of pivotal confidential information), crunch numbers and understand their relevance so that clarity and simplicity can be achieved during the negotiation, reflect on elements pertaining to an existing relationship seeking to decide how to "play it out" in the round, and discern "signal" from "noise" to prioritize across multiple interests.

Certain fact patterns are particularly helpful in honing this essential skill. The problems in this section specifically challenge a team's preparation. These scenarios teach participants to anticipate calculations, specific numbers that pertain to specific outcomes, and very particular details that become relevant during the session. Use one of these fact patterns in higher-level competition, to discern who can prepare comprehensively for a mediation or negotiation.

Tell teams to bring a pen and paper when engaging with these problem questions, as well as any additional relevant documents. Expect these rounds to lurch and judder, rather than running smoothly. Teams must pause to make calculations and thoroughly understand the material.

Logic Tree Example

Using the fact pattern from the "Trouble in Paradise" case, we will outline a logic tree from the perspective of the responding party. These questions are examples of using follow-up questions to obtain more information from your opposing party. These questions are not exhaustive, and no matter your level of preparation for a mediation/negotiation you should always expect some surprises.

First, identify the unknowns about the requesting party. Some examples include:

- Whether the opposing party knows what was wrong with the wine and if so, whether such an event can be avoided in the future.
- What quality controls exist internally at CF to ensure products are up to Bellissimo's standards.
- Whether CF values Bellissimo as a partner to the same extent that Sam values CF.
- How CF wanted to move forward with their business partnership following the expiration of the contract, and whether the events that unfolded have changed their perspective.

Next, prepare questions related to each unknown to ascertain the other party's strengths, weaknesses, and interests. Watch for answers that lead to "sub-questions" that build upon the first question. Here is an example:

- Unknown: what was wrong with the wine?
  - Question: Do you know what may have occurred to make the wine unsuitable for consumption?
    - Possible Answer: Yes, and it was a one-time oversight/mistake/error.
  - Follow-up questions: How can you assure Sam that such an event will not occur again? Can you increase quality assurance? Can you guarantee that this will not happen again? Has CF made any internal changes since this occurrence?
    - Possible Answer: Yes, and it was an oversight/mistake/error on the responding party's end.*

* Occasionally, the other team's confidential information includes facts relevant to you that you did not know. Remember to prepare for that possibility.

  - o Follow-up questions: When did you learn about our error? How can we improve the line of communication and ensure this does not happen in the future?
    - ■ Possible Answer: No, we have no information about what occurred to spoil the wine.
  - o Follow-up questions: What quality control methods are in place at CF? How can we be confident something like this will not occur in the future? Do you have any educated guesses, as experts in the food and wine distribution field, as to what may have happened?

After exhausting these questions and answers, the results should lead the team to logical options: writing a formal apology to Sam from CF, appropriately compensating for the effects of the incident, and negotiating a future contract that amends and updates all four points of the contract.

A team should prepare for each identified unknown and craft workable solutions designed to answer both parties' needs. Using our example, during the discovery period, the team may determine that CF is happy with the current business arrangement, admits *some* liability for the spoiled wine, and is worried about their future business profitability and reputation. You believe Sam will demand a payment of $1 million in damages. Offer instead a payment arrangement in the form of a product discount, ensuring CF retains profitability, until the agreed-upon amount is paid in full. In exchange, you could require Sam not to make CF's written apology public, helping CF uphold its reputation for excellent quality food and wine.

Remember that there is no final binding agreement until both parties at the table agree on everything. Feel free to table certain discussions and amend solutions as new options come to light. While doing so, keep track of how each solution impacts your desire and ability to accept an alternative solution.

Chapter Two Problems

Ride'n Dirty

General Information

A contract rider is a supplemental document to the principal performance contract that a musician sets as criteria for a performance. It typically consists of two parts: the hospitality rider and the technical rider. The former is a list of comfort requests the day of the show, such as food and drink. A technical rider delineates details about equipment setup for the show such as lighting, sound systems, and pyrotechnics. In the 1970s, a well-known rock-n-roll band famously included a "bowl of M&M's, no brown ones" in their hospitality rider. The reasoning behind such a specific request is this: if a venue has not read the hospitality rider, then they likely did not read the technical rider, which poses a serious risk to the performance and audience. Since then, many performers embed oddly specific requests in their riders.

Last year, a young artist named Freddie Redder released his first song online on various streaming platforms. Within forty-eight hours, the song had over 100,000 downloads, and it was picked up by international radio stations by the end of the week. Inspired, Freddie released more tracks that he had prerecorded and was delighted when those also performed exceptionally well. Less than a month later, a mid-sized recording label, Lex Records, contacted Freddie to sign a record deal. Thrilled, Freddie immediately signed the contract and worked at writing his first album as a signed musician. He finished and released the self-titled album within six months and enjoyed massive success worldwide. Freddie Redder was invited to music events, conducted various television interviews, and quickly became a beloved new artist in the music scene. Lex Records informed Freddie that his contract required him to tour his album in Europe and North America for one year. Freddie enthusiastically agreed.

The tour management team quickly coordinated a headlining tour beginning in Los Angeles, California, and ending in Rome, Italy, from January to November of this year. A performer at heart and wanting to define himself as not just a musician but a *showman*, Freddie requested that the tour include highly technical elements, including a laser light show and a pyrotechnical grand finale. His label agreed. The technical rider, amongst other things, stated the following:

> **Ceiling:** The height of the ceiling should be twenty-five feet minimum, thirty-three optimum. There shall be no decorations, cables, or debris placed above the stage.
>
> **Pyrotechnics:** The Talent shall provide to the venue six pyrotechnic devices to discharge during the Grand Finale at a height of sixteen feet.

His hospitality rider included numerous requests, including:

> **Snacks:** Potato chips with assorted dips; peanut butter cups; pretzels; and assorted nut mix (NOTE: ABSOLUTELY NO ALMONDS).

All venues agreed to the entirety of the rider. Tickets went on sale for the tour and sold out within thirty minutes. Everything was in place and on schedule, and Freddie left for California on January 3, of this year. His first few shows went off without a hitch; his fans adored the intricacy of his performance and Freddie felt energized and excited for each concert. He finished the American West Coast and was steadily performing his way through middle America towards New York, New York. On the night of his tenth show, Freddie arrived late and rushed through soundcheck, claiming he needed time to conduct his preshow ritual. The staff at the venue asked that he stay to run through his "grand finale," but Freddie refused and walked off stage until he was set to begin his performance.

The opening band went onstage on schedule and finished their set around 8:30 p.m. Freddie was set to begin his performance at 9:30 p.m. By 10:30 p.m., Freddie had still not appeared, and the audience became highly irritated. Luckily, Freddie went on stage at 10:45 p.m. and performed most of his set without any issues. However, disaster struck during Freddie's final song.

Freddie's grand finale included a huge laser display, eight pyrotechnic devices discharging simultaneously, and thousands of streamers releasing into the crowd from the ceiling. Unfortunately, when the devices released their fireworks, items around the stage caught on fire. The scene turned into complete chaos, with thousands of people scrambling to escape the venue and Freddie himself fleeing into the night. While some minor injuries were sustained, no one was seriously injured from the event.

When Freddie was located several hours later, he was seriously shaken by the events. He told the tour manager that the screams of his fans were haunting him, and that when the fire started, he feared for his life. Tearfully, he told the manager that he could not in good faith continue the tour as planned. He understood that this would come with the loss of a lot of money, but he felt the malfunction was his own responsibility arising from his plan to include a highly technical final song. Freddie became inconsolable, had a meltdown, and just kept groaning, "My fans . . . my fault" over and over.

Lex Records had to cancel the rest of the tour and issue refunds to all ticketholders. They released a statement on social media which simply read "due to technical difficulties, Freddie Redder's remaining tour dates must be rescheduled. All ticketholders will receive full refunds within sixty days." Soon after, Lex Records reached out to the venue demanding $3 million in damages for lost sales. A venue representative reached out to Lex Records and requested that the parties first try mediation/negotiation to settle the matter. Lex Records agreed. The venue's owner and Lex Records' founder and CEO will attend the session, represented by their respective legal counsels.

RIDE'N DIRTY
REQUESTING PARTY INFORMATION

Requesting Party: The Venue's Owner

In the twenty-five years that you've owned and operated this concert venue, you have never once had an issue even close to this magnitude. You're devastated and worried that, should blame for this disaster fall on you, the public's trust in your venue will be ruined and you'll have to close indefinitely. A few days before the concert, the owner of Concert Giant, a chain of event stadiums approached you. The chain made a first and final offer, to buy you out for $2.5 million by the end of the month. This would cover 75 percent of Lex Records's claim, and you have sufficient insurance to cover the rest. However, you hate the idea of relinquishing your beloved venue. You will do everything in your power not to take the Concert Giant deal but worry you will be forced to if you cannot come to a reasonable solution with Lex Records.

You spoke to the venue manager about the evening in question and received much valuable information. The night of the concert, Freddie showed up late and intoxicated. Upon returning backstage after his soundcheck, he completely melted down that the snacks were not to his liking. Despite the rider requiring an assorted nut mix with no almonds, Freddie insisted he wanted no cashews instead. He trashed the room and threw the bowl of nuts directly at the venue manager, who was trying to calm him down. The venue manager suffered a slight concussion from Freddie's outburst. As a result of his behavior, there was no time to test the pyrotechnic devices before showtime.

You reviewed videotapes of the concert and noted a series of errors. One of the pyrotechnical devices shot fireworks over twenty-three feet, which was higher than specified by the technical rider. You also saw that the malfunction threw the timing of the show off and fireworks were still discharging when the streamers fell. Your guess is that when the streamers released, a few caught fire, which then ignited various set décor. In your lawyer's opinion, because Lex Records provided the pyrotechnic devices, the liability lies with Lex Records completely. However, after further inspection you have ascertained that the venue's ceiling is tall enough to have accommodated the pyrotechnic devices' range of fifteen feet; it measures twenty-four feet exactly. It should have been plenty to accommodate the pyrotechnic device, but you worry that this will implicate you further should the issue proceed to litigation.

You are also angry about Freddie's treatment of your venue manager. You will never book another concert for a musician signed by Lex Records unless the label guarantees that a violent outburst will never occur again. Your venue is the largest in middle America and a necessary tour stop between the West and East Coast. It would be a logistical nightmare for Lex Records to skip your venue for all tours moving forward.

Your main interest is fixing your reputation in the public eye. The reaction on social media is split between blaming Freddie Redder and the venue. Given his immense popularity, some of Freddie Redder's fans have begun antagonizing you directly. Most recently, you've received death threats against you and your family, which has terrified you. You believe that it will not stop until Freddie "calls off" his fans on social media. You hope that despite the differences at the table, the Lex Records representative will request this of Freddie from a humanitarian perspective. You also believe this will restore some of the reputational damage you've sustained.

You are willing to pay some damages to Lex Records if it will solve this dispute. Your venue is expensive to operate but profitable, and you've budgeted about $1 million to be paid over a one-year period.

You are confident that you have excellent bargaining power in the course of this negotiation, as Lex Records has seven scheduled dates for the upcoming year. However, if necessary, you will undertake litigation to avoid selling your venue to Concert Giant. You are ready to protect yourself and your venue at all costs.

RIDE'N DIRTY

Responding Party: Lex Records

In the aftermath of the disaster, you and your team have been feeling a bit guilty about your treatment of Freddie. A young and amateur musician, he barely had enough time to process his fame before you whisked him off to various promotional events. Although he tried to remain calm, you suspect that the concert may have driven Freddie over the edge. At first, he was evading his manager's calls, but now you have spoken to him directly and learned his version of events. According to Freddie, he arrived late to the venue and was already highly stressed as he had not yet overcome his stage fright. After a curtailed soundcheck, he went backstage to calm down before the show. He became upset over snacks laid out in the dressing room and addressed it with the venue's manager. Trying to resolve the issue took much longer than expected and Freddie was an hour late for his show. He reports that the show went well up until the grand finale, but he cannot recall much else. From some online videos, it appears that one of the pyrotechnic devices misfired and shot over twenty-three feet. Prior to starting the tour, the equipment manager informed you that the devices were outdated and advised you to purchase a new set for the show. You had planned to retire them after this tour, but you must now replace them quietly and immediately. While this ordinarily would render you liable for the damage and lost future revenue, the ceiling height requirement stipulated by the technical rider should still have accommodated the height of the misfire safely. Members of Freddie's band suspect that the venue had some decorations from a previous concert strung to the ceiling that would have been a fire hazard and thus the reason for the catastrophe. Therefore, it is your counsel's position that the venue could in fact share liability for the event.

You and Freddie have agreed that after a three-week rest, he should be ready to resume the tour. You have not yet issued ticket refunds. You based your demand for damages off the ticket price of $15 x 200,000 (tickets sold for shows that had not occurred). You plan to restart the tour with the Amsterdam show, three weeks from now. In this case, you will only have to refund 70,000 tickets. You would like the venue to compensate you accordingly and as soon as possible so that you can continue to operate your business profitably.

Whether the public will welcome Freddie's return to the tour is a different issue entirely. You worry his fans will fear a similar event happening and request refunds. You must reassure the public that this was a one-off event that will not be repeated. You believe that the venue publicly accepting liability would restore the public's confidence in this tour. You are willing accept a lower damages payment in exchange for a public declaration of liability from the venue. You cannot afford to dissolve your relationship with the venue altogether, as its location is an essential stop in most American tours. It would be a logistical nightmare to rebook the seven upcoming tours you have planned for the next year.

Now You SeeMe, Now You Don't

General Information

The president of Garvaria has put forward a bill to implement a new system of tracking citizens with a mandated national app, "SeeMe," that must come standard on all Garvarian phones. This mandatory app would be automatically installed on all smart phones. The bill was put forth as a groundbreaking new security measure that would ensure the safety and security of Garvarians by allowing police to respond more quickly to potential crimes (among other benefits). SeeMe has pinpoint location tracking, access to phone cameras, and can obtain data when government or police deem it necessary to do so. The bill is at the final stage of reading currently in the Garvarian House of Commons and Garvarians expect the bill to become law this week.

The bill has a large and vocal opposition. Protesters argue that this infringement on freedom is a huge government overstep. For the last five days protests have overcome the streets of Garvaria. A large convoy of cars and trucks has camped outside the Garvarian House of Commons for the last five days. Thousands are participating in the protest, with signs, loudspeakers, and microphones. While the protests have been peaceful, the temperature is visibly rising and the Garvarian parliament worries that it will reach a boiling point.

What started as a fringe movement is no longer such. The Garvarian protesters enjoy widespread and growing support from other countries, and protest against the bill has gone international. This has emboldened protesters, who refuse to leave the streets leading to the House of Commons until the bill is dropped.

Garvarian citizens are split over their support of the protests. Those who live near the House of Commons complain that their essential roadways are blocked, forcing them to endure traffic jams and obstructed access to essential services. Further, some citizens complain of protesters heckling them as they walk or drive by the House of Commons.

The Garvarian president has failed to engage with the protest movement, either blatantly ignoring questions in the media or in the House of Commons about the protests or dismissing the legitimacy of the movement, referring to the protesters as a "fringe group." They have even resorted to name-calling, referring to the protesters in an interview as "idiotic," "individualistic," and as "fake Garvarians."

In the previous five days there has been only one violent event of note: an isolated fight between a protester and a counter-protester. Spokespeople for the "Cancel SeeMe" protest movement have publicly disavowed this fight, stating that "violence has no place at this protest, and we will not stand for it."

The media within Garvaria is divided on the issue of the protests. Some are calling for the police to break up the protest and forcibly remove the protesters from in front of the House of Commons. Those supporting the protest claim that it is the citizens' right to protest and that the police have no just cause to break it up.

The local police have patrolled the protest site over the last five days. There have been increasing complaints that the police have been heavy-handed in dealing with the protesters. Some videos have surfaced of officers being physical with the protesters. One video shows a tall, red-headed officer grabbing a protester by the throat and yelling at them to stand down. This video has gone viral, circulating widely amongst protest supporters, who claim that this exemplifies the overreach of government power they have been complaining about.

Today, another concerning video has gone viral. The video shows a crowd swarming around the same tall, red-headed officer, who is cursing and motioning aggressively. The crowd disarms him, begins to carry him off, and then the video cuts out. The police officer's colleagues failed to contact the officer for the last two hours. The police and the government worry that the officer has been captured by angry protesters.

The Garvarian government has reached out directly to spokespeople from the Cancel SeeMe movement and demanded immediate mediation/negotiation, to which the spokespeople agreed. They meet at the table with the primary objective of determining the whereabouts of the missing officer and ensuring his safe return home. At the table they will also discuss the future of the protest and how the two sides can come to an agreement over the future of the bill.

Now You SeeMe, Now You Don't
Requesting Party Information

Requesting Party: Garvarian Government

Officer Adric has gone missing for three hours. The Garvarian police are outraged and are calling for an immediate and violent response. They wish to send a highly armed search team to find their comrade and bring him back to safety immediately. This is a viable option; your espionage branch believes they have located a mobile trailer where the officer is being held.

However, extracting Officer Adric would require some door-kicking and violence on the part of the police and could result in the captors harming Adric in the process. Cooler heads in the government argue for a more methodical approach. Sending an armed team into the protest camp would be political suicide and destroy the already feeble public image of the government and police—never mind risking Officer Adric's personal safety. At the table you must determine the location of the officer immediately and negotiate his prompt return to safety. If the spokespeople fail to deliver, your government will have no choice but to send a team in to retrieve Officer Adric.

After securing the officer's safe return, your government wishes to bring him to justice for his poor conduct. Likewise, you wish to bring his suspected captors to justice. If this was in fact a kidnapping, those involved must be prosecuted to the full extent of the law. As this situation has become public, you want to manage the government's public image to the best of your ability. You want to leave the table with a public statement from the Cancel SeeMe movement apologizing for the incident and taking full responsibility.

Moreover, the government is aware of a video that was uploaded (and since taken down) of Officer Adric being extraordinarily violent towards an elderly woman. The video saw the officer striking her and taunting. Civilians have filed multiple complaints against Adric for being overly aggressive. If those who carried the officer off knew of this horrific act of violence, Adric may face vigilante justice by the hands of his captors. As such, the video must be kept a secret, at least until Officer Adric has been returned.

Further, the government is concerned that the roadways to essential services such as the local hospital are being blocked. The fastest route to the hospital uses Dolomoti Road, which is currently occupied by protesters. You must leave the table with the spokespeople's assurance that Dolomoti Road will be cleared as soon as possible.

You also need to develop a plan to get the protesters to stand down within a week. Otherwise, your government will appear weak. While you cannot guarantee any changes to the bill or amendments, you are able to alter the proceedings of the final bill reading to include a speech from the spokespeople for Cancel SeeMe and their participation in the question period at the end of the bill reading. You will only offer this option if the spokespeople will guarantee the end of the protests.

You must act quickly and effectively at the table today to ensure the safety of Officer Adric and the reputation of your government.

Now You SeeMe, Now You Don't
Responding Party Information

Responding Party: Cancel SeeMe Spokespeople

You were blindsided when you heard that a police officer had been captured at the protest. In your eyes, the protesters had done a great job up until this point of avoiding violence and confrontation. Other protest organizers told you the officer is being held in a mobile trailer near the center of the protest (on Dolomoti Road) and protected by two guards. You spoke with one of the guards over the phone ten minutes ago who assured you the officer had not been harmed. The guard seemed frightened and said he "doesn't know what to do." You could hear the captured officer cursing at his captors. You instructed the guard to not harm the officer in any way; he agreed with this. When you asked him to release the officer he said, "Not until our message is heard! And I won't give him up to no cop." You believe you could go to the trailer (perhaps with the assistance of an undercover policeman), retrieve the officer, and bring him back to safety. As a spokesperson of the movement, you are respected enough that the officer will not be harmed while he is with you.

The officer should be released as soon as possible, and the capture should not in any way be associated with the spirit of the protest. This would undermine the message entirely and make the protesters look like nothing more than a band of thugs.

You are keenly aware that some police officers have been overly aggressive while policing the protest. In exchange for release of the captured officer, you require the Garvarian government to ensure that not only will Officer Adric be investigated for his behavior, but to guarantee a general inquiry into police conduct as a whole at this event. You will be sure to approach this topic delicately in light of recent events.

You recognize that this protest, while necessary, is proving to be quite cumbersome for locals to work around. You are willing to take some measures to clear the main roadways so that locals can better access necessary services. However, you are adamant that the protest will not stop until the voice of Cancel SeeMe is heard. Protesters are offended by the president's comments about them and refuse to give up until the government hears their case. You want the government to scrap the bill entirely.

You have the reputation of the protest movement and the wellbeing of an officer of the law at stake. You must approach the conversation at the table today with careful consideration.

Big Fish, Little Pond

General Information

The town of Qualia is small and rural, with a population under 2,000. Qualia is a renowned hunting and fishing hotbed and the townspeople and indigenous population have a passion for both. They often joke, "don't tell anyone about Qualia" because they want to keep their little piece of paradise as quaint and secluded as possible.

Qualia has enjoyed a quiet existence for many years with limited interference from big business. Most residents are ranchers and farmers but some supplement their income through the hunting and fishing industries. Resident experts offer guided fishing trips on the nine local lakes. The residents gripe about the extra traffic in the summer but begrudgingly recognize the summer fishing industry as a necessary source of income for many. Even with the guided fishing trips growing more popular with "out-of-towners" the nine lakes remain relatively remote and undiscovered.

That is, until two years ago. Billionaire business tycoon Sam Sevro of the esteemed Sevro family learned of Qualia as a location for a profitable land investment. Sam purchased 70 percent of Qualia's ranch land, amounting to 40,000 acres in total. Contained within the purchased ranch land are seven of the town's nine fishing lakes. Despite the size of the purchased land, the actual worth of the investment is one of the smaller assets in the Sevro family portfolio. Things were never the same for the fishers of Qualia after Sam purchased this land. Owning all the land surrounding the seven lakes, the Sevro family claims they now also have exclusive ownership of the seven lakes themselves. Sam has publicly stated that the Sevro family plans on developing the lakes into exclusive fishing resorts all under Sevro family ownership. Townspeople who spent their lives and supplemented their income fishing these lakes were told they no longer had legal access to seven of the nine regional lakes.

Claiming legal ownership over the lakes is uncertain. There is no legal precedent that would allow the purchase of a lake. However, access to the lakes requires crossing Sevro family land. Sam has made it clear that nobody can trespass upon this land unless given express permission by a member of the Sevro family. Therefore, anyone attempting to access the lake would effectively be trespassing.

As one can imagine, Sam's ownership claim of the lakes did not go over well with the residents. Townspeople and indigenous people alike disregarded posted signs and continued fishing the seven lakes now within the Sevro family's property. The Sevro family resorted to fencing off many of the popular access points on their land, blocking private roads, and charging fishers with trespassing, all of which furthered discontent among the locals.

In response to the Sevro family's land purchase, avid fishers and numerous other interested parties formed an organization called FFQ ("Fisher's Fellowship of Qualia"). FFQ went public with their grievances against the Sevro family and have received support from surrounding indigenous populations, local government, and the Department of Highways. FFQ's blog post titled "Not Yours to Take" has been gaining popularity and has been reposted over 3,000 times so far. The blog post is likely to garner widespread support for FFQ's fight against the Sevro family. In an attempt at good faith and with the possibility of a court trial on the horizon, Sam, on behalf of the Sevro family, sent a letter addressed jointly to the Township of Qualia and FFQ requesting immediate mediation/negotiation. The organizations agreed and elected to send Mayor Valki to represent both the Township of Qualia and FFQ's interests at the mediation/negotiation. As the mayor of Qualia and an avid fisher, Mayor Valki is uniquely positioned to advocate for the interests of both groups. Sam, Mayor Valki, and their councils meet at the mediation/negotiation table with the goal of settling this dispute before it gets even messier.

Big Fish, Little Pond
Requesting Party Information

Requesting Party: Sam Sevro

The Qualia ranch land may be one of the smaller assets in the Sevro family portfolio, but it is turning out to be more of a headache than the family bargained for. Sam didn't think twice about purchasing the rural land; it was quite a bargain at $6 million. Sam knew the development potential for the land was immense. The Sevro family stands to make a serious profit, offering luxury tours of the lakes over the summer months to fishing enthusiasts and snowmobiling in the winter. The family invested half a million dollars updating the ranch houses as guest accommodations, but it has been difficult to find good employees with all the negative press.

At the instruction of the family, Sam ensured all seven lakes were under the family's sole ownership. Sam felt morally uncertain about privatizing the lakes and asked the family on multiple occasions, "Can anyone really own a lake?" Sam did not get a satisfactory answer, only instructions to proceed with securing their investment, and thus, continued fencing off many of the popular access points on their land, blocking private roads, and charging fishers with trespassing. Sam felt these measures were the best way of maintaining sole ownership but felt that the blocking of through roads may be an overstep of the Sevro family's ownership rights.

The Sevros never thought blocking access to the lakes would result in the outrage that it did. The negative publicity from FFQ and their blog post threatens the family's other, more lucrative investments. This bad publicity must be stopped from spreading before it creates a public relations disaster. While the Sevros could easily afford going to court, doing so would undermine their reputation built over generations of being ethical and philanthropic businesspeople. Moreover, it is uncertain whether the court would side with the Sevro family in privatizing the lakes, and it is likely the family would receive a censure for blocking off the roads going through their property.

Further complicating the situation is some trouble within the Sevro family. Sam's sister Matea Sevro is a second-year university student who recently converted her major to indigenous studies. Matea is appalled at her family's disregard for indigenous land rights. In family conference calls she has threatened to publicly announce her consent for the local indigenous population to cross the Sevro land to access the seven lakes, effectively making the access points public once again. Sam hopes this is an empty threat, as Matea would be undermining her family's interests by doing this. But if Matea is serious, this would be disastrous for the Sevro's new investment. Sam believes this is family business and will not reveal Matea's rebellious threats unless explicitly asked.

The Sevros are not willing to be pushed around by the FFQ or the townspeople. They are open to granting some limited lake access to locals but want to maintain their exclusive fishing tour business. Sam can offer, as an incentive, the family's interest in employing more local fishing guides. The Sevro family's guided fishing tours could potentially contribute over 25 percent of the Qualia economy and employ up to 30 percent of the locals seasonally. The Sevros would also be willing to grant conditional access for townspeople and indigenous populations (partially to appease Matea) to the most popular of the seven lakes, Rochdia Lake, and will negotiate access to one or two others if necessary to bolster their public image. Yet, the Sevros are firm on maintaining exclusive ownership of the majority of the seven lakes. You must balance this ownership interest with restoring their reputation in the community and their business reputation more broadly.

Big Fish, Little Pond
Responding Party Information

Responding Party: Mayor Valki

Mayor Valki has the tough task of representing multiple parties at the table. In the mayor role, there are financial concerns to address as well reputational concerns. The town needs industry to give the locals more employment opportunities. Having a family like the Sevros as investors in Qualia land could bring a much-needed boost for the town economy and increase Mayor Valki's reputation in the process. However, both as an avid fisher and the mayor, Valki has a keen sense of what taking the lakes away from local fishers would do. Besides worrying about the ethics of private lake ownership, Valki wonders about the precedent this would set elsewhere. Could billionaires own all the lakes in the world simply by owning the surrounding land? Moreover, the townspeople love fishing, and these seven lakes are the locals' pride and joy, especially Rochdia Lake, which produces the biggest trout in the region nearly every year. People are complaining most about lack of access to Rochdia Lake.

The mayor also knows that there is a lot of money in the fishing industry. The small-scale fishing tours that Qualia locals guide account for about 15 percent of the Qualia economy and employ 20 percent of the population seasonally. Valki figures that a well-organized fishing tour business could easily increase those figures. Taking this industry away completely would be bad news for the economy and the pride of the Qualia people. The mayor should ensure that the Sevros will employ the local fishers to guide their tours.

The FFQ is a volunteer organization, and the town of Qualia hardly has any money. The mayor is amazed at how influential a blog post can be, however, and will use the town's good relationship with the "Not Yours to Take" blog author to drum up some press if it ever becomes necessary. A notable big city lawyer read FFQ's viral blog post and contacted Valki about getting involved. Among other things, this lawyer mentioned that blocking essential roadways is illegal, despite the roadways existing on private property and being maintained by the property owners. If a roadway deemed essential connects to one of the seven lakes, then the Sevros can no longer claim sole ownership of that lake. Not all roadways the Sevros blocked could be deemed essential, but at least three of the seven lakes have roads that a court would likely view as essential. The lawyer is keen to take the Sevro family to court and happy to provide her service pro bono. This lawyer also mentioned that a Sevro family member has reached out to her and indicated that they were interested in helping the FFQ's cause.

The mayor doesn't really trust big city lawyers and doesn't know whether to believe the lawyer's claim that a Sevro family member is willing to help the FFQ. The mayor would rather seal the deal alone. Moreover, the mayor knows that the town and FFQ would collectively be outspent at court and risk losing access to the seven lakes altogether. But, if the Sevro family proves difficult, the mayor might be left with no other choice but to accept the services of the big city lawyer. The mayor wants to leave the table:

1) Gaining access for locals and indigenous populations to a minimum of three of the seven lakes (including Rochdia);
2) Securing jobs for the local fishing guides who are currently unemployed over the summer; and
3) Maintaining a reputation as a strong leader who advocates for their townspeople and the indigenous population.

Currency Collapse

General Information

Outdoor goods supplier Asteria Life Co-op (ALC), located in the country of Asteria, and outdoor action and adventure store Flow, located in the neighboring country of Bulgos, have enjoyed a successful business relationship for the past five years. Asteria and Bulgos have different currencies. Asteria uses their native asters while Bulgos uses buls as their currency. The companies signed a contractual agreement for ALC to be Flow's exclusive provider of kayaks for redistribution. The agreement is binding for ten years. The agreement is as follows:

1) ALC will supply kayaks and will receive payment at a locked price of 250 buls per unit from Flow. ALC will be responsible for sourcing their own materials, manufacturing, and providing their product at this price point.
2) ALC will be the exclusive provider of Kayaks for Flow for the ten-year duration of the contract.
3) ALC will be required to deliver all ordered kayaks to Flow within a month of the order placement.
4) Flow will sell their kayaks for no more than 600 asters during the agreed-upon contractual period.
5) The parties will be required to follow the terms of the contract for the allocated period; the contractual obligations by either party may only be deemed void under conditions of bankruptcy.
6) Breach of any of the contractual terms can render the contract void.
7) The contract being rendered void will trigger an immediate renegotiation clause.

Both parties were quite pleased with their partnership agreement. Before their partnership, Flow had trouble finding a good kayak manufacturer. Flow had no access to carbon fiber within Bulgos. ALC on the other hand has a proven manufacturing system in-house that they use to create all their carbon fiber products, such as kayaks, paddleboards, skis, snowboards, and more. In the years following the inception of the Flow/ALC partnership, kayaking has become far more popular in Bulgos, and kayak sales currently represent 65 percent of Flow's net sales, making them the leading kayak provider in Bulgos. ALC supplies to multiple stores, with Flow being one of their largest clients.

Issues in the partnership began last year when political disaster struck Asteria. The sitting Asteria Prime Minister Darlene Jums was near the end of her leadership term. With low prospects of reelection, Prime Minster Jums publicly began pedaling misinformation about her rival political party as well as claiming that members from within her own cabinet were conspiring against her reelection. In a televised press conference, Jums strongly hinted that her true supporters should take action to prevent this fictional illegitimate conspiracy. The press conference stirred up Jums's loyal supporters and a group of 100 individuals "stormed the parliament" and forced entrance into Asteria's capital buildings. Fortunately, no politicians, citizens, or law enforcement officers were harmed in the mayhem, however "the storming" had disastrous consequences for the Asteria economy, collapsing the aster. Previously held at equal value to the bul, the political instability dropped the aster to half the value of the bul. Since the storming, the aster has stayed at this poor value due to the instability of the coming prime minister elections. This currency devaluation has notable consequences for ALC and Flow's partnership. Flow is bound under the current contract to paying 250 buls per unit (the equivalent of 500 asters) for their kayaks while they can charge no more than 600 asters (or 300 buls) for the product. Wanting to reevaluate their agreement given the change in circumstances, the Flow CEO has asked to meet with ALC CEO for mediation/negotiation immediately. Both CEOs will be joined by their legal counsel at the table.

Currency Collapse
Requesting Party Information

Requesting Party: Flow

When you became the CEO of Flow a year and a half ago, you wanted to create stability for your employees and pay competitive salaries with excellent work-life balance. Unfortunately, the recent events have undermined your ability to uphold that dream for your employees and colleagues. The currency fluctuation has forced you to cut the salaries of your employees by one-third and decrease the hourly rate of your retail employees to minimum wage. Several people on your team are working overtime with no pay to try to strategize a way to increase the profitability of the business during this time of currency instability. Your top priority in this meeting is to renegotiate a contract that will ensure your employees never have to experience such stress again. In your capacity as CEO of Flow, you have unsuccessfully attempted to contact the ALC CEO for over two weeks. You initially thought this currency debacle would be simple to resolve. However, after two weeks without contact from the ALC CEO, you fear a bigger problem. While Flow is selling other outdoor action and adventure items, the loss it is taking in kayak sales is chipping away at the bottom line. You are worried that the continued political instability in Asteria and the possibility of Asterians reelecting Prime Minister Darlene Jums could drop the aster value even further. You need the CEO of ALC's opinion on this. At this rate, Flow will go bankrupt in five years but will seek alternative means of dissolving the contract and looking for other suppliers before allowing this.

Your business overhead costs incurred per kayak is 60 buls. As such, Flow is losing ten buls for every kayak sold. Flow must renegotiate the contract so they are making a minimum of fifty buls after costs but would prefer to make closer to 150 buls per kayak. If Flow can profit 100 buls per kayak, you will be able to pay back the lost wages of your employees within one year. If you can increase the profits to 150 buls, you will do so within seven months. If you can only convince ALC to allow you to profit fifty buls per kayak, it will take two years to pay back these wages. You fear that such timelines will result in a mass exodus of your top performers. Therefore, you must try to convince ALC's CEO to allow the highest profit margin possible or risk losing most of your team. Whether this arises by way of raising kayak prices, currency change, or other means, this is a necessity for Flow before leaving the mediation/negotiation table today. An option for nullifying this currency debacle is renegotiating the contract to be based off digital currency. Digital currency Dige Coin has become far more popular around the world, is more stable than either country's native currency, and is widely accepted by most venders. Dige Coin's current value is equal to the aster.

You would also like to renegotiate the term of the contract that puts a maximum cap on the retail price of the kayaks. As the demand for outdoor gear rises, your other competitors have significantly increased the cost of their kayaks. Though one might imagine your competitive prices would make your product *more* popular, a significantly cheaper product signals to the consumer that the material and quality of the item is lower as well. You and the CEO of ALC know very well that this is not the case, but you need to raise the cost of the product to match the changing trends.

Although the contract stipulates that ALC must be the sole provider of kayaks for the ten-year contractual period, you have recently been approached by Outfitter Outdoors Inc., who claims to be revolutionizing watercraft sports. They have innovated the kayak and canoe into a new hybrid product coined "the CanYak" that promises the stability and durability of a canoe with the swiftness and control of a kayak. After consulting with your counsel, they are satisfied that this product is sufficiently unique to be deemed an altogether different product, and you would not be in breach of contract to stock this item. However, CanYak has not come to market yet and so there is uncertainty about how it will be received by the public. Luckily, this puts you in a unique position to negotiate an advantageous contract between Flow and Outfitter Outdoors Inc., which you will pursue if ALC will not meet your interests at the table today.

Currency Collapse
Responding Party Information

Responding Party: Asteria Life Co-op (ALC)

In your youth, kayaks were completely cost prohibitive. You dreamt of joining your secondary school's paddling team but were never able to realize that dream because kayaks were never affordable for the lower-middle class. When you became the CEO of ALC, you promised yourself and your team that ALC's mission is and will always be to keep the outdoors accessible for all. As such, ALC is committed to preventing their vendors from increasing their sale price. This is a part of your core beliefs as an individual and business mogul. Moreover, you are naturally averse to the greed of big business and consider it exploitive for any distributer to be making more than 60 buls per kayak sold. You suspect that the CEO of Flow's true desires will be to capitalize on this opportunity to renegotiate the contract to maximize profitability. You have little respect for such opportunistic businesses. However, you also recognize that Flow is an important distributer for ALC, making up 30 percent of its total income. With paddling sports on the rise, you want to renew the contract between ALC and Flow for another ten years. Although you will be diligent to ensure that any new stipulations of the contract negotiated at the table today will not prohibit consumers from accessing kayaks, you also do not want to exploit Flow with an unfavorable contract. Therefore, you are open to renegotiating certain terms. However, you want to keep the spirit of the original contract as you feel it reflects ALC's business values.

You are still upset about the business dealings that occurred two years ago after the prices of carbon fiber rose due to a worldwide shortage. The cost of manufacturing kayaks increased, and Flow's CEO refused to renegotiate the terms of their contract. As a result, ALC did not accrue any profit manufacturing kayaks for Flow for six months. This made for a total loss of 108,000 buls as follows:

> Under usual conditions, ALC profits 60 buls per kayak. Flow orders an average of 300 kayaks per month for a total of 1,800 kayaks for six months, totalling a loss of 108,000 buls.

As a condition of renegotiating the contractual terms and as a symbol of good faith for the occurrence two years ago, you would like Flow to make reparation payments of 80 percent of the lost profits. You also want a new contract clause that protects ALC from such an occurrence in the future. The currency devaluation and resultant economic collapse in aster is causing problems for some of ALC's other distributers. ALC is not making nearly the revenue that they had been making previously. It is important to not lose any distributer during this time of political and financial instability. ALC's CEO recognizes that the issues in using multiple currencies was bound to occur at some point. The CEO has heard some of the younger employees talking about encrypted digital currencies. Though the CEO does not know much about these new currencies, ALC is open to dealing in these currencies in the future.

Just Keep Digging*

General Information

The neighboring countries of Opeia and Mireia share a rich yet tumultuous history. The two nations once lived in synergistic harmony as sister countries, where Opeia provided quality textiles and livestock in exchange for Mireia's bountiful harvest from its richer soil. This arrangement was successful for many years, and the countries shared open borders with free movement and rights of settlement. The election of Opeian President Harold Nazgar changed things. He was jealous of Mireia's superior soil, capable of producing much better and more plentiful produce. He embargoed Opeia's exports to Mireia, refusing to lift it for the entirety of his presidency. Mireia subsequently refused to provide any exports, and the people of both nations suffered. After two years, civil unrest plagued the streets, and any person from one country found in the other was subject to violence and abuse. The president of Mireia, Sholeh Niti, insisted on establishing distinct borders and citizenship laws to protect her people and limit infiltration of Opeia's citizens, who were known to attack Mireian villages at random. She attempted to negotiate with Harold, but he proved to be as volatile as his actions and demanded a border that significantly encroached on Mireia, cutting the land by about 50 percent. Sholeh negotiated a better deal and they drafted a border which only cut through about 25 percent of Mireia.

Before the agreement could be finalized, disaster struck. A volcano located on the border of the two countries erupted, destroying several small villages and covering much of the land in ash. Each country suffered hundreds of casualties including their respective presidents, and briefly set aside their conflicts to grieve and remediate the damage. No one, however, remediated the land near the "border" as it remained unclear in which country it lay, and the people were tired of conflict.

Eventually, each country appointed a new president. While talks of the border were tabled, anger and contempt remained. The embargos were never officially lifted, and it became an unspoken rule that free settlement from one country to another was no longer acceptable. Citizens still traveled over the borders, though, to trade their own products with other villagers, which became a frequent occurrence. This arrangement has existed for several hundred years.

Last year, renowned Opeian archaeologist Micah Reneaux organized a team to excavate the volcanic site, which was left largely untouched after the eruption. They wanted to learn more about the history of Opeia during Harold Nazgar's presidency, as the history books are hugely biased and only written from generational stories, passed down through time, about the peoples' suffering. They sought to understand how the people lived during that time and began a dig in the area that was encrusted in volcanic ash. After several weeks, the team made an incredible discovery. The village they unearthed was rich with artifacts perfectly preserved below the rubble. Hundreds of detailed journals documenting life in that time, as well as pottery, art, tools, and more were uncovered. Micah's team immediately informed the Opeian government of its discovery, which quickly declared that the site fell within its jurisdiction. Naturally, the Mireian government intervened as well. They claim that the initial discovery site and many others are within the unofficial Mireian borders and therefore all artifacts belong to their government. The current president of Opeia insists that the past agreement between presidents Nazgar and Niti should stand, which undoubtedly places all sites within its borders. The outraged Mireian president publicly proclaimed that Micah's team began the excavation without the appropriate permits. Archaeological digs without the required permissions are a serious offense in both countries, and if this accusation is true, the team faces serious jail time. The Mireian president declared that if review of the circumstances reveals that any of the sites are within Mireia's borders, they will press charges to the fullest extent of the law. The Opeian government and its people are keen to protect Micah's team from prosecution, and Mireia's people feel that Opeia is attempting to rob them of treasures which rightfully belong to them. This situation threatens to incite civil unrest once again after centuries of quiet peace.

In an act of good faith, the president of Opeia made a personal phone call with the Mireian president. After a heated discussion, it was clear that Mireia demanded the following:

A) A declaration that all the sites fell within Mireia's borders and jurisdiction;

B) An immediate cease to the dig by Micah's team, to be replaced with a Mireian archaeology team;

C) Ownership rights to 90 percent of the artifacts discovered so far; and

D) Ownership rights to all subsequent artifacts discovered.

The discussion infuriated the Opeian president. They refused to accommodate any of these demands and are uninterested in further discussions with Mireia. Luckily, a few days after the conversation, a Mireian representative contacted the Opeian president's office and requested mediation/negotiation over the terms and conditions of the discovery. Both parties think that undertaking such a discussion is an excellent idea, and representatives from each government will be accompanied by counsel to discuss the pressing issues at hand.

Just Keep Digging
Requesting Party Information

Requesting Party: Mireia

After hanging up the phone with the Opeian president, the president of Mireia immediately regretted the content of their conversation. They have always personally felt that Mireia was disrespected in the times of Nazgar and Niti, and they let their emotions overtake them during the conversation. They are sorry about the unreasonable demands made and embarrassed to have represented their country so poorly. Restoring the two countries' harmony would solidify them as one of the best presidents in many centuries, and this is the opportunity for which they have longed. They are willing, therefore, to negotiate with Opeia and retract their previous demands. Nonetheless, the president has made it resoundingly clear that they must not feel taken advantage of, as Mireia was all those years ago.

The president has instructed you that the first thing they would like addressed in the session is the centuries-long export embargo. If you can start the mediation by officially lifting the embargo, this symbol of good faith between the countries will encourage a favorable outcome of the whole session.

Two substantive issues must be addressed during the discussion: where the border lies between the countries, and the disposition of the artifacts thus far discovered. The Mireian president has secretly disclosed to you that Niti negotiated a better deal between the countries only because she blackmailed Nazgar with evidence of his affair. They assert that she acted out of desperation, and you must try to uphold that agreement or negotiate a better deal. A border honoring the original agreement between Niti and Nazgar will give Mireia claim to 50 percent of the artifacts. However, accepting this agreement will be highly controversial for your people. Honoring the second (but unfinalized) agreement would only give Mireia claim to 40 percent of the artifacts. This is unfavorable to you. You are more concerned with receiving more of the archaeological artifacts than with where precisely the border is lain. You have been instructed to negotiate a border which cuts through no more than 16 percent of Mireia, which would technically only give you rights to 15 percent of the artifacts. In exchange, you will request at least 51 percent of the artifacts. You feel this is reasonable, considering Opeia's role in the oppression and suffering of the Mireian people. You plan to pardon Micah Reneaux in exchange for a higher percentage of the artifacts as well. In a brief before your session, the president informed you that Reneaux is currently in custody of the Mireian government, awaiting the result of this discussion to decide whether he will stand trial. You are not sure if Opeia is aware that Mireia is currently holding Micah in custody, but the Mireian president is only willing to release him if you make a favorable deal with Opeia. If not, then Mireia will prosecute Micah to the fullest extent of the law. However, the fact that he is in custody without the express knowledge of Opeia threatens to offend the Opeian representatives and dissolve the entire negotiation. You must manage this with great tact and reassure them that this is not done in bad faith, but rather to protect Mireia's interests during the course of your negotiations.

The president plans to open a historical museum to honor the Mireians who lost their lives during the eruption and place all artifacts there to honor their ancestors. You believe this entitles you to a larger portion of the items discovered so far, as well as the right to continue the excavation yourselves. The museum is in the country's capital, several hundred miles from the dig sites. This will bring desperately needed tourism into Mireia. The embargo on Mireia's exports has depressed Mireia's economy, since the country is isolated from the rest of the world and Mireia is unable to export perishable goods anywhere else. The people of Mireia still blame the Opeian government for their difficult way of life, especially since Opeia's textile exports have flourished in the past few decades. To avoid civil unrest, it is crucial that you honor Mireians with this museum. Therefore, you have been instructed to negotiate that Mireia retain sole rights to continue archaeological discovery in this area. You hope Opeia's representative will be amenable to a fair arrangement between the parties that honors the centuries of the exploitation that Mireia endured. You have full settlement authority with respect to all aspects of this contract. Perhaps a joint project is the first step towards reconciling the countries and cultivating a more fruitful future.

Just Keep Digging
Responding Party Information

Responding Party: Opeia

The president of Opeia is still heated from the last conversation they had with the Mireian president. A fiercely loyal Opeian, the demands offended them deeply and must be addressed first during the mediation. The president insists on a written apology from the Mireian president and will be unamenable to any of their requests without one. Your counsel has advised you that political figures are often extremely hesitant to produce apologies. Therefore, it is crucial that you handle this request delicately yet sternly. You know the Opeian president needs a personal rather than public apology, and that he wants the Mireian president to admit that they were disrespectful during the course of their last conversation. If you secure an apology that meets these parameters, you can move forward with the rest of the mediation.

Opeia has been left largely unscathed by the embargo placed on the country's exports, as its quality textiles are easily sold abroad for profit. By contrast, you know Mireia has suffered and blames Opeia for the hardship. You hope to leave any animosity between the countries behind at the end of this mediation. The primary concern following the written apology is protecting your esteemed archaeology team. Micah Reneaux approached the president a few months before the dig but failed to mention that the sites would encroach on Mireia. Although the president was upset with Micah, they have urged you establish how much of the discovery site falls within Mireia's borders. If you take the position that the original agreement between the presidents is upheld, then 50 percent of the artifacts technically belong to Mireia. If the unfinalized agreement is accepted, then only 40 percent of the discovery sites were within Mireian borders. The president knew Micah's team lacked even Opeia's necessary permits, and although it *is* a serious offence in Opeia, the president is unconcerned with enforcing such archaic laws.

You have no information on Micah's current whereabouts, though there are theories that they have gone into hiding to avoid standing trial. Should the Mireian government prosecute Micah and team, you fear it will ignite a new era of civil and political unrest. You must avoid this at all costs. Therefore, the Opeian president has instructed you to accede to some of Mireian president's demands in exchange for pardoning Micah. It is up to you when to mention this condition.

After both parties agreed to mediation, the president divulged to you, during a private conversation, that Micah had discovered a redrafted contract between Presidents Nazgar and Niti. It is unclear whether the contract is genuine, but analysis of the signatures suggests that it is. The discovery of this document is a secret held only between you, the Opeian president, and Micah. Under this contract, the division between Opeia and Mireia are much closer to equal. The border drawn between the countries cuts through only 10 percent of what is considered Mireia, but the total land mass is roughly equivalent. In good faith, the Opeian president is willing to honor this agreement between the parties. However, he would naturally prefer to negotiate a border that gives Opeia more land mass and a claim over many of the artifacts. If you can negotiate a border cutting through 18 percent of Mireia, it will give Opeia legitimate claim to 55 percent of the artifacts. If you can only negotiate to 15 percent, it gives Opeia claim to 40 percent, and if you settle on the 10 percent border, Opeia will only have claim to 25 percent. However, the offer is dynamic, and you should consider negotiating a higher percentage of the artifacts for a border that encroaches less on Mireia. This must be balanced with the pardoning of Micah.

The president wants to continue conducting archaeological digs in the border area of Opeia and Mireia. The president plans to sell the artifacts at auction and use all proceeds to restore the damage from the volcanic eruption. This will create a vast historical site between the countries that could bring in considerable tourism to the two countries, from which both could benefit. The president feels this entitles them to a significant portion of any subsequent artifacts discovered. They insist that any team sent to excavate the site must employ Opeians, in the interest of fairness and good faith. You hope Mireia's representative will be amenable to a fairer arrangement. You have full settlement authority with respect to all aspects of this contract. Perhaps a joint project is the first step towards reconciling the countries and cultivating a more fruitful future.

CHAPTER THREE

TEAMWORK

If a team is presenting as client and counsel, then their relationship should come across as colleagues with a strong working relationship. To do this, counsel must learn their client's expressions and body language, and/or develop a system of verbal or nonverbal cues so counsel can jump in when the client becomes overwhelmed or uncertain. Counsel should be apprised of the client's business undertakings and be able to clarify any points the client makes that are poorly phrased or not in their best interests. A great way to practice teamwork is to use fact patterns that center on a contract or legal document. This creates a clear division of talking points for the discussions and your team can practice speaking only on the material that is relevant to their individual role.

If engaging in a negotiation competition, teams are often comprised of two legal counsels (either senior and junior counsel or co-counsels). In this case, division of responsibility is of utmost importance. As co-counsel, enter the negotiation understanding who is responsible for which items in the agenda; your team will appear more organized—crucial to scoring well in the teamwork category. If you are training a team presenting as junior and senior counsel, the same principles apply. We recommend assigning one member as senior counsel and the other as junior counsel for the duration of competition so that the roles are clear and there is minimal risk of interrupting or contradicting one another.

There are a multitude of ways that teamwork can manifest at the table. A team must identify their respective roles and not waver from those roles during a negotiation/mediation; this clarity fulfills role expectations. For example, if opposing counsel asks a client a very pointed or otherwise aggressive question, it is incumbent on the lawyer to shield their client by interjecting. Accordingly, the client's role is to advance their interests the vast majority of the time, and the lawyer's is to limit themselves primarily to process-related matters. Deviating from this role division increases the likelihood of poor teamwork. Teamwork also requires the lawyer (not exclusively, but most often) to use various available tools such as breaks, caucuses, mediator intervention, the agenda, etc., to support the client throughout the round in a way consistent with the client's interests. This includes managing the momentum at the table, capturing progress when it is achieved, and managing progress consistently as it culminates towards a potential outcome.

Skilled teams also show effective teamwork by openly strategizing during a round or by openly demonstrating support. Execute these skills during the open session or during a caucus. Effective teamwork also means displaying discipline, restraint, and mutual support while executing your strategy/plan at the table. In practical terms, this takes the form of skillful interventions to manage the flow and nature of the discussion. It is very fact-specific.

Chapter Three Problems

Pollution Solution

General Information

Arana is a large tropical island that boasts lush forests and biodiversity and that has flourished without any external influence. The entire country operates in harmony with nature and each other. Each village has plenty of land for agriculture and raising livestock. There is a local market each week where all the people gather to barter and trade goods such as produce, textiles, meat, and medicinal salves. Laborers offer services in exchange for goods as well. Although the people are technically poor monetarily, there are few needs or wants throughout the country as the people live simply and rarely get sick—likely due to their excellent diet, active lifestyle, and natural approach to medicine.

A few months ago, things began to change for the village of Ethos, located on the southern coast of Arana. Many of their domesticated animals began acting strangely—they would wander far away or would collapse suddenly and without warning. Local veterinarians provided medicines that treated the symptoms but were unable to diagnose them with any known disease. Some improvements were made for a few weeks, but then they got worse and began to die. Around this time, the Aranian people noticed that their health was deteriorating as well. Their teeth became discolored or rotted, and many experienced difficulty breathing. Again, the doctors tried to ward off symptoms and again were only successful for a few weeks. People began suffering from sudden onset asthma attacks, and some developed flu-like symptoms. The situation became desperate when it was discovered that crops were suffering from root rot and were largely inedible. Although some of the inner-island vegetation remained healthy and available for foraging, this vegetation is not sufficient to sustain the population of Arana for longer than eight weeks.

A week after the people of Ethos became ill, four men from the village of Echos, forty miles up the River of Arana (which runs through the entire island and supplies all the people with fresh water for drinking and irrigation of their agricultural land), appeared in Ethos in search of help. They reported that eighteen months ago, people from a foreign country arrived by air to Echos in search of some land to purchase. They met with the leader of Echos and promised riches in exchange for a small portion of land at the base of Arana Mountain (where the streams that feed into the River of Arana originate). Out of curiosity, and because an arrangement like this had never been made in Aranian history, the leader agreed. Within weeks, several workers arrived by air and ship to Echos and constructed a large-scale industrial factory. The factory opened ten months after the initial agreement. The factory now manufacturers clothing and ships it to other countries. The people then described how, although initially the arrangement worked well, the situation changed two months ago—an illness spread amongst the animals, people, and agriculture—just like in Ethos. The situation has progressed in Echos, and people are becoming gravely ill and malnourished, along with most of the livestock dying. Allegra, leader of Ethos, instructed that the travelers be fed and treated with the best available medicines and selected three strong villagers to make the journey upstream back to Arana Mountain to investigate. When they arrived, they surveyed the land surrounding the factory and discovered a drainage pipe that was continuously pouring liquid into the river. They reported that it was dark blue in color and had a foul odor. A sample was collected and brought back to Allegra (who practices traditional medicine) where it was analyzed and confirmed as causing the illness plaguing Aranians. Allegra demanded that the manufacturing of the factory be halted immediately, which it was.

A few days later, Aidan Viber, who manages the factory, came to Ethos to reason with Allegra. They said that a legal agreement had been made with the leader of Echos and that while production had been halted out of respect, they had every intention of returning to the factory and continuing production immediately. They refused to answer any questions about what liquid was being poured into the river, but adamantly rejected the idea that it was causing the illness spreading throughout Arana. Aidan said that the plan was to continue production indefinitely, even ramping it up to twenty-four hours per day to make up for lost profits. Upset and feeling helpless, Allegra contacted the chief from a village on the mainland for help. Word quickly spread about the situation on Arana, and people became enraged. A campaign began that called for the immediate shutdown of the factory and for aid to be sent to the Aranians in the form of fresh food, water, medicine, and feed for the livestock. People identified the clothing manufactured and boycotted it, refusing to shop at any stores that stocked their products. Aidan returned to Ethos begging for forgiveness. Initially, Allegra refused to meet with him, stating that he had offended Ethos and Arana deeply. However, Allegra later announced that to remediate the damage done to the country, they would meet with authorities from the factory to negotiate how to move forward. The parties will meet in a neutral location for a mediation/negotiation session. A lawyer from the mainland has volunteered to accompany Allegra pro bono to protect their interests in the mediation and has assured Allegra that should mediation be unsuccessful, their office would be willing to represent Allegra in litigation pro bono as well. Aidan Viber will be present in the mediation with their in-house counsel.

Pollution Solution
Requesting Party Information

Requesting Party: Allegra

You are horrified by the events that have unfolded in your beloved country of Arana these past few months. Watching your people and their livelihoods suffer has been harrowing, and you shudder to think of what could unfold if action is not taken immediately. Aidan Viber threatens legal action if you do not lift the ban on production. You scoff at the threat. There is no official court in Arana; Aidan Viber's contract is effectively useless. Additionally, you hope Aidan and their counsel adhere to Arana's procedures for settling disputes, which must be explained at the outset. Under Aranian tradition, any issues regarding remuneration are saved for the final points of discussion. This is in the interest of finding common ground and a fostering a shared desire to focus on "*sumi lum arda*," Aranian for "the things that matter." Also, the requesting party often invites the responding party to offer their opening remarks first, as a symbol of good faith. This is the first Aranian dispute with an international party, and you hope your traditions will start the discussion on a collaborative note.

Your heart aches for the suffering of the people of your country and you must, at all costs, protect their health and livelihood against Aidan Viber and the factory. When you received the initial water sample from the Aranian river, you conducted traditional experiments that revealed chemicals in the water capable of causing extreme illness. This was all the evidence you needed to suspend the operations of the factory. However, upon the advice of your counsel, you sent the sample to the mainland to be tested in a laboratory. The report confirmed the presence of indigo-4 in high volumes. Upon further research, you learned that this substance is a textile dye, which when ingested in large enough quantities can cause fatigue, fainting, and pulmonary infarction. There are no recorded deaths related to the ingestion of indigo-4. Your anger was reignited, and you immediately met with your counsel to discuss your options. They informed you that from a strictly legal standpoint, Arana has no formal laws that govern the disposal of hazardous waste. However, Aranian law allows a leader to pass a law at any time with the express permission of all other leaders in the land. Additionally, with the approval of at least 51 percent of the Aranian populace, you may apply said law retroactively. You have already received permission from the other leaders (there are four total and no chiefs currently) to pass a law banning the dumping of any waste materials anywhere on or within a 100 km radius of Arana. If the discussion proves unsuccessful, you will hold a vote amongst Aranians to decide whether the law will apply retroactively. Regardless, you wish to pressure Viber to provide you with a plan for removing any waste products during the factory's operations.

A few weeks ago, you met with the leader of Echos to understand the agreement she made with Viber. She said three people approached her and identified themselves as representatives of the factory who wanted to purchase a piece of Aranian land. They represented to her that the land would be used discreetly, and that it would be an honor to be the first non-natives to own a piece of Aranian property. They offered 8,000 runas in exchange for this land. Runas are completely useless in Arana—Aranians do not use currency but operate off a barter system. However, the leader liked the representatives and so agreed to the sale. When presented with the contract, she informed them that she could not read English, but they assured her it was only symbolic to signify the deal was official. Later, once the factory was built, she overheard one of the representatives boasting that the budget for the land was 80,000 runas. After hearing the story, you feel that the conduct of the representatives was clearly predatory, and you expect to obtain 90,000 runas for such due to coercion and the misrepresentations made to the leader. You also maintain that this renders the contract completely null and void in any jurisdiction.

When brainstorming a solution to this problem, you were contacted by Valentina (a large retailer that the factory supplies) with an offer. They said that there were looking to completely transform their company into an affordable and sustainable clothing retailer and would be willing to continue operations in Arana with your express approval. Valentina is by far the largest of the three clothing retailers on the mainland (along with Warrenco and Avaya Clothing Co) and plans to buy out both companies by the end of the year. You were initially hesitant to approve the continued operations of the factory. After speaking to some Aranians, you discovered that many want to work in exchange for runas. They dream of exploring the world beyond Arana and never had the opportunity because of a lack of work in Arana. They have asked you to advocate for their right to be employed by the factory and you are happy to oblige. After understanding that laborers from the mainland earn thirty runas per hour, you would like the opportunity for Aranians to be employed at a rate of twenty-five runas per hour. The decreased amount is due to a lack of practical experience, but you expect the rate to increase annually until the same hourly rate is reached.

The health of Aranians has improved drastically since receiving humanitarian aid. However, you want to restore balance to Arana for those who still wish to live in the traditional manner. Therefore, you must be guaranteed that the new hazardous waste laws will be meticulously adhered to, and that you have the right to suspend operations any time if you feel that the factory (or any of its representatives) is acting unethically.

Pollution Solution
Responding Party Information

Responding Party: Aidan Viber

As the manager of the Aranian factory, you feel backed into a corner by everyone involved in this dispute. Your boss is rightfully upset about the circumstances that have unfolded, you face public backlash that threatens to shut down the factory, and the leader of Ethos has only begrudgingly agreed to speak with you. It is important to you personally to build a good rapport during this discussion and make it resoundingly clear that you are simply the middleman of this controversy.

Well, that's almost the case. In fact, when your boss Leandre Saccio (a very wealthy business mogul) brought up a new venture manufacturing and distributing clothing around the world, you felt this was an amazing opportunity to finally earn Leandre's respect. You spent weeks scoping out potential locations and stumbled across the little-known country of Arana. You felt it was the perfect, discreet location for this factory. You instructed three people to travel to Arana on your behalf and purchase a suitable piece of land for 80,000 runas (the currency from the closest country in the mainland). They convinced the leader of Echos to accept only 8,000 runas in exchange for a piece of land at the base of the mountain of Arana where the factory now resides. In your view (which your lawyer agrees) this was a legitimate legal contract that binds the parties, and there is a written document to prove it. If a suitable agreement cannot be made to satisfy Leandre, you have full authority to pursue litigation.

The first few months of the factory's operations went smoothly. Clothing was being supplied at a steady rate to the mainland and distributed directly to three of the largest retailers there: Warrenco, Valentina, and Avaya Clothing Co. The margins were considerable, and the business became profitable quickly. However, Warrenco advised you that they needed to cut costs as the demand for "fast fashion" items grew. They informed you that unless you dropped the prices for clothing by 50 percent, they would withdraw and take their business elsewhere at the end of their contract (in two months' time). You were able to meet this request, but Avaya Clothing Co quickly caught wind of the price drop and demanded the same. Losing any one of these three retailers would ruin the profitability of the business—therefore, you were obliged to meet Avaya's demands. Unfortunately, the current employees are all citizens of the mainland and will not work for less than thirty runas per hour. You had no choice but to obtain much cheaper textiles and dyes to keep profit margins at 10 percent. These products produce a lot more liquid waste, which was not accounted for in the original construction of the factory. Employees were instructed to dump the excess waste down the drainage pipes, and you planned to find a better solution at some point—but have taken no action to that effect. However, you are not convinced that ingesting these dyes causes the illness described to you by the Aranians. In fact, if sufficiently diluted by the river, few effects should be experienced at all. Therefore, you must discover what tests the leader conducted on her sample from the river. Additionally, your lawyer informed you that Arana has no laws that govern proper disposal of hazardous waste, and although you come to this mediation in good faith, the fact remains that no laws have been broken to date. Nevertheless, all three retailers are now threatening to withdraw their business at the end of their contracts† if the matter is not settled promptly.

When you originally approached the leader asking for forgiveness, you were confident that without her express (and public) approval, the factory would be shut down by the end of the month. However, one of the largest global retailers, Valley-Mart, has contacted you with an interest in initiating business with you. This company has a reputation for unethical business practices, opting for factories with the lowest wages, cheapest textiles, and most hazardous dyes on the market. If you enter into a contract with Valley-Mart, you will likely be compelled to adopt these practices to keep your margins at 10 percent, and your public reputation will be ruined. Even worse, the offer Valley-Mart sent you includes a non-negotiable clause that they can extinguish the agreement at any time. You have not spoken with Leandre about this offer yet since it is so high risk.

You plan to continue operations in Arana, since it would be a considerable expense to relocate elsewhere. It will be much simpler to do so with the permission of Allegra, and so you are willing to undertake some action to gain her approval. You plan to offer to continue the monthly supply of fresh water, produce, and medicines. The cost is 4,000 runas per month and would give Aranians peace of mind. In exchange, you hope that Allegra will publicly withdraw her complaint, which will reinstate business as usual. You would also like to recover the cost for suspended production. The company is set to lose 40,000 runas by the time of the mediation, and your plan is still to increase production to twenty-four hours per day until the 40,000 is recovered. It will take fourteen days to do so, and if it goes well, you would like to continue operations at this rate. You are not sure how Allegra will respond to this request, but Leandre Sacco has given you full settlement authority to reach an agreement that is amenable to both parties. Leandre does not wish to tarnish their name, and therefore has given you a budget of 100,000 runas for settling this matter to ensure that the factory remains operational and profitable.

† All three contracts end in two months but will auto-renew for another year unless explicitly withdrawn.

Lights, Camera, Action!*

General Information

Gullywood, a new age style of western cinema based in Bashville, Mennessee, has swept the nation for the last few decades. Known for accents thick with the iconic southern drawl and epic cowboy fugitive shootouts, Gullywood is set to become the largest grossing film industry to date with its next three upcoming movies.

Of all the film starlets and sweethearts starring in these projects, none is better known or higher paid than Eliza St. James. Her breakout role in *Tracing a Fugitive* eight years ago featured her as a southern belle with a heart of gold trying to find her father, a cold and calculated outlaw (played by none other than Gullywood A-lister Hendrick Thomas). She played a few follow-up roles that cemented her as Gullywood's sweetheart. A few years later, her smash hit *Breaking the Saddle* reimagined St. James as a manipulative harlot—the role proved that Eliza is as sensual as she is sweet, and as talented as she is beautiful. Eliza St. James is under pressure to outperform herself in each subsequent role she undertakes.

Eliza is currently under contract at Sunrise Studio, one of the largest and most profitable production companies in Gullywood. Six months ago, Sunrise agreed to loan Eliza St. James to Wolfbrain studio for a three-part movie series titled *Mother May I.* Under contract, Wolfbrain is to pay Sunrise Studio $5 million per film at the outset for loan of Eliza and 15 percent of the profits of each film. Wolfbrain is also obliged to provide Eliza with all her requests during and between filming. The first movie concluded filming within five weeks. It is rumored that Eliza's performance as a single mother battling her internal sociopathic tendencies in a desolate town is harrowing. Film critics predict Eliza will be nominated for her first Golden Statue Award for this role, and that the trilogy has potential to smash records at the box office.

A few days after filming wrapped, Morel Minue, executive at Wolfbrain, called Bazil Brooks, an executive at Sunrise, claiming that they wanted to dissolve the contract immediately and replace Eliza with another Gullywood starlet, Connor Germaine. Confused, Bazil hung up on Morel, assuming that they were just in an emotional rage—a common occurrence in the film industry. One week later, Sunrise Studio was served with a Notice of Intention to Terminate from Wolfbrain. The reasons cited include:

1) Inability to perform the stipulations of the contract;

2) Unreasonable demands; and

3) Refusal to perform expected obligations.

All executives at Sunrise were blindsided by the notice—except for Bazil Brooks. She informed Wes Anthony (leading executive at Sunrise) of this misunderstanding and was promptly fired for misconduct. Wes immediately called Morel to apologize for the miscommunication but explained that their position was that the reasons for

Notice to Terminate were not sufficient to dissolve the contract and still expected performance. Morel rattled off about a lack of professionalism and a failure to disclose the true nature of the arrangement and threatened litigation before hanging up the phone. Not wanting another Gullywood scandal, Wes contacted their public relations agent, who advised mediation/negotiation as a pseudo-legal mechanism that would allow for the resolution of the dispute discreetly and without prejudice. Wes Anthony emailed Morel requesting to mediate/negotiate, which was accepted. The parties will meet in a neutral location accompanied by their in-house counsel.

Lights, Camera, Action!
Requesting Party Information

Requesting Party: Wes Anthony

You are not completely certain what complaints Wolfbrain will have about the arrangement, but as far as you're concerned, business is business. In fact, Wolfbrain approached *you* about loaning Eliza St. James—a deal that Sunrise hesitated to make. Though loaning actors to other production companies is not uncommon, Eliza St. James is an exception. Her presence in a film alone is capable of filling millions of theater seats, and a three-part trilogy means that Sunrise cannot cast her in its own productions for at least a year. After some negotiation, Sunrise finally agreed to the arrangement because of Wolfbrain's offer of 15 percent of the revenue from each film. Typically, a movie starring Eliza St. James nets around $300 million. This means that Sunrise is set to make at least $135 million this year without lifting a finger. With talks of Golden Statue Awards swirling, and rumors that the film will smash box office records (the highest-grossing movie in Gullywood to date made $900 million) you are confident that both Wolfbrain and Sunrise are set to profit immensely from this arrangement.

You can't say that you particularly disagree with Bazil Brooks's interpretation of Morel's phone call. Executives and talent in the industry act insufferably from time to time—that's the nature of the business. You also won't tolerate petty complaints about a few tantrums thrown by an A-list celebrity. Wolfbrain should handle these situations with more professionalism, and you are irritated about sitting through this mediation/negotiation. While you admit that Bazil could not necessarily have known the gravity of Morel's phone call, someone had to take the fall for the miscommunication; firing Bazil was more symbolic than anything. As cutthroat as this industry is, Bazil Brooks is one of the best in the business. Bazil's eye for talent and artistic intuition is unparalleled by anyone you've seen in your twenty-plus years of experience in Gullywood. You don't want to offend Morel, but you'd like Morel's blessing to rehire Bazil.

You heard through the grapevine that Connor Germaine is the niece of a Wolfbrain executive. Nepotism runs rampant in Gullywood, and most movie stars come from a long and established line of fame. That is fine. What is not tolerable is an executive undercutting this lucrative contract to replace Eliza with an irrelevant breakout actor. You suspect that the reasons listed in the Notice of Intention to Terminate are a bogus attempt to replace Eliza with Connor. Your public relations firm advised that replacing Eliza would bring bad press—something you cannot afford after her most recent scandal. Some time ago, Eliza was rumored to be getting a little too close to Hendrick Thomas during the filming of *Tracing a Fugitive.* Hendrick is fifteen years her senior and married to Charlotte Lafleur. Hendrick is also signed to Sunrise Studios, and allegations that he was straying from his marriage (Hendrick and Charlotte are a Gullywood "power couple") would have cost him considerable favor with the public. You spoke Eliza and Hendrick privately, and they both assured you that it wasn't true—they simply have good chemistry and respect for one another. Actors are generally honest about the truth behind a scandal; it is in their best interest, so the publicist can handle it. In response, Sunrise sent Hendrick and Charlotte on a long vacation to a popular island to stimulate good press about their marriage and get the attention off Eliza and Hendrick. Arranging their travel, hiring private paparazzi, and paying the major media outlets to only post stories of their picture-perfect marriage came at the high price of $5 million. Sunrise also has several movies in the shooting and editing phase and only one in theatres—meaning very little revenue until the premier of *Mother May I.*

You want the current arrangement between Sunrise and Wolfbrain to be successful. Wolfbrain is a newer company trying to establish itself within the film production industry. A recent meeting of Sunrise Studio executives decided that Sunrise will refocus its projects into something more niche—silent Gullywood films. Obviously, this is a huge risk. Sunrise has several other A-list actors (Peyton Grace, Aspen Adams, Alessandra Evans, Phillip Antonio) that you are eager to loan to Wolfbrain. This would cement Wolfbrain as a production giant and bring Sunrise considerable passive income while it focuses on passion projects.

You've spoken to Eliza as well—she is thrilled with her performance in *Mother May I,* convinced that it is her best yet. She informed you that she wants to really break free from her public image as Gullywood's sweetheart for good and believes this trilogy is the best way to do so. You are willing to speak with Eliza to address Wolfbrain's concerns and ensure that the contract is upheld and the subsequent films are successful.

Lights, Camera, Action!
Responding Party Information

Responding Party: Morel Minue

Working with Eliza St. James has been the worst experience of your career. Hardly a day went by during production that Eliza did not make an unreasonable demand, show up late, or throw a tantrum on set. Wolfbrain was initially willing to pay any amount to dissolve the contract between itself and Sunrise just to get rid of Eliza for good. That is, until everyone watched the most recent cut of *Mother May I.* Eliza's performance is dazzling—you've never seen anyone convey a story the way Eliza does, and everyone is confident that several Golden Statue Awards will be awarded to Eliza and Wolfbrain on award show night. Everyone at Wolfbrain is tentatively willing to continue the arrangement, but you've been given the large task of resolving this dispute before moving forward.

Eliza's behavior on set must be addressed. She was consistently hours late, which caused huge expense in artificial lighting (to simulate daytime hours) amounting to $10,000 per day alone. She demanded exorbitantly expensive bottles of champagne every other day and a private helicopter on two occasions, forced the costume department to replace the entire wardrobe for the film, and insisted her trailer be replaced with a more luxurious option. In total, Eliza's demands alone cost $250 million. Since Wolfbrain is a newer company, you worry whether you will recover the total cost of production. On the night after filming wrapped, Eliza approached you privately in your office. During your meeting, she said that she was not a fan of Donahue Adler, who plays her love interest in *Mother May I.* She wanted Donahue replaced with Hendrick Thomas, her co-star in *Tracing a Fugitive.* You knew this was a bad idea—Eliza St. James was recently rumored to be having an affair with Hendrick, who is married to Charlotte Lafleur (another A-list actor). Already concerned about the profitability of the project, you did not want to bring any negative press before the premier. You pointed out that Hendrick had played Eliza's father in their previous film, and the pairing as lovers would not be believable. Eliza threw a full-blown tantrum. She ripped pictures from the wall, knocked over a shelf filled with antiques, and poured coffee all over your desk. You'd finally had enough. You yelled a few profanities and forced her out of the office. To make matters worse, Connor Germaine barged into your office a few seconds after Eliza left. She overheard the entire conversation and knew that Eliza was in love with Hendrick Thomas. She said, "The press will be *very* interested to know that the innocent Eliza St. James is in love with a married man! Unless, of course, you cast me in a leading role." Desperate to avoid this scandal, and fed up with Eliza's behavior, you called Bazil Brooks and told her you wanted Eliza gone and replaced with Connor. Now that you've cooled off, you'd rather give Connor a different project to lead in, but the studio does not have a production in the works. You must formulate a plan to either keep Connor Germaine quiet or mitigate the damage if her story breaks out.

After you heard Bazil Brooks got fired, you called her up to personally apologize. The two of you had a lengthy discussion, and you want to offer Bazil a job with

Wolfbrain. Bazil is the best in the business. Bazil's eye for talent and artistic intuition is unparalleled by anyone you've seen in your experience in Gullywood. You don't want to offend Sunrise, but you'd like their blessing to hire Bazil.

As far as the contract, you fear that Eliza's behavior will prevent you from making any profits at all. To continue the current arrangement, you want a ceiling on Eliza's personal requests of around $500,000. This is the only way you will be able to honor the current agreement—otherwise, you will have to withhold the $6 million for the two sequels. You also want Sunrise to pay $15,000 for the damage Eliza caused to your office.

Though you've yet to discuss it with Eliza, you'd like Sunrise to sign off on a few scenes with nudity in the final film. You don't know if Sunrise Studios will agree (considering Eliza's reputation as Gullywood's sweetheart) but you believe it's necessary for the storytelling of *Mother May I.* You are confident that with some negotiation, the arrangement between Wolfbrain and Sunrise Studios will end profitably and with a few well-earned Golden Statue Awards.

The Latest Buzz*

* This problem was used in the semi-final round of the Transatlantic Negotiation Competition.

General Information

The Ostrov Museum of Art (OMA) is located in the Republic of Ostrov, a tiny country in the Northern Hemisphere. Despite its small size and remote location, Ostrov has recently gained international recognition for the OMA, which features the beloved works of the Ostrov-born artist, Pieter Petrov. His most famed exhibition, first presented five years ago, was titled *Honeybee*. All the pieces drew inspiration from the insect. Petrov's art features a range of unique mediums and techniques, but none is better known than his sculpture titled "Propolis," a seven-foot golden statue of a queen bee. Though the piece is undoubtedly remarkable, featuring brilliant wings of stained glass and a body of bronze and gold, what is most astounding is its weight. Pieter miraculously produced this piece to weigh only fifty-five pounds, in an innovative technique that he promised to reveal at the end of the one-year exhibition. Tragically, Pieter suddenly died five months short of the deadline, before he could disclose his secret. While the Republic of Ostrov grieved the loss of the beloved artist, the mystery of his technique drew world-class curators, artists, traders, and art buyers to the previously obscure country to tour OMA for the honeybee exhibition.

Two years ago in May, the country of Argento opened its largest museum to date, called the Argento Museum of Classics (AMC). For generations, Argento has been regarded as the world's epicenter for art, music, and culture. The most famous works of humankind usually reside in one of Argento's iconic museums. The AMC is a meticulously curated display of the most astounding pieces from artists such as Straude Monet, Victor Ban Gogh, and Henry Matisst.

Shortly before opening, the AMC began curating for its first year-long exhibition, titled "New Age Classics," featuring artists of this century. AMC approached OMA for loan of Propolis to be displayed as the final piece in the exhibit. OMA initially declined to loan its most cherished artwork. AMC offered OMA a handsome sum and assured the safe return of Propolis after the end of contract. Knowing the display would increase its reputation and draw even more tourism and wealth to Ostrov, OMA eventually agreed.

The agreement between AMC and OMA stipulates:

1) An initial payment of US $200,000 to OMA;
2) Transportation costs for Propolis paid by AMC ($10,000);
3) Monthly installments to OMA for $200,000 x12= $2.4 million;
4) In the event of reparable damage to Propolis in transport or during display, AMC to pay OMA $70,000;
5) In the event of irreparable damage of Propolis in transport or during display, AMC to pay OMA $10,000,000; and

6) The parties must explore alternative dispute resolution before litigating any disputes that arise during the contract.

AMC successfully transported Propolis without any issues and began to display her in June two years ago. The people flocked to marvel at the brilliant sculpture.

Art historian and professor Dr. Alexei Martial became obsessed with the piece, trying to understand how Petrov accomplished this work. Rumors say he spent hours and consulted many sculptors, goldsmiths, and historians trying to recreate the technique. Overall, the exhibit was a renowned success for both AMC and OMA. As the months passed, OMA began to anticipate the return of its prized possession, investing in a beautiful solarium extension to display Propolis permanently.

On February 4th, of last year, AMC was scheduled to close at 3:00 p.m. in anticipation of its national holiday on February 5. Martial made one last visit to Propolis before leaving on a three-month sabbatical. On February 6, upon reopening of AMC at 9:00 a.m., the staff immediately noticed that Propolis was missing. AMC began a frantic search for Propolis, hoping she had been moved for cleaning, but she was not found. Security footage of the museum malfunctioned at 1:00 a.m. on February 5. An initial inspection of AMC did not reveal any indication of foul play, and Martial was seen leaving the premises at 2:45 p.m.—he was the last visitor documented in the museum. AMC alerted local authorities and OMA immediately, and there is an ongoing theft investigation to find Propolis.

There is massive speculation relating to the missing sculpture. The public is devastated at the loss of the piece of history, and questions of how Petrov accomplished this amazing feat remain unanswered. AMC has received severe backlash for not installing extensive security measures, given Propolis's remarkably light weight. "#cancelAMC" has circulated on various platforms, and several artist's estates and museums have demanded the return of their cherished works. OMA claims that the missing sculpture is a result of AMC's gross negligence. They are threatening immediate legal action for breach of contract and are demanding $17.8 million: $800,000 for the remaining four months that Propolis was on loan, $10,000,000 for "irreparable damage" to Propolis as a result of the loss, $1,000,000 for loss of future revenue to the museum, $1,000,000 for the investment into the new solarium, and $5,000,000 for the loss of an irreplaceable asset. AMC has requested negotiation under section 6 of the contract. AMC and OMA will be represented by their legal counsels, with full settlement authority.

The Latest Buzz
Requesting Party Information

Requesting Party: AMC

This is a disaster. The loss of Propolis is devastating, and the lack of measures taken to keep Propolis secure is humiliating. A thorough search of the entire museum left very few clues as to what could have happened; every door was locked and none of the motion sensitive cameras revealed any unusual movement—at least up until 1:00 a.m. on February 5. The only information you have comes from the security guard on duty that night. He reports arriving for his shift at 11:00 p.m. and walking through the premises as standard procedure. He is certain that he saw Propolis in place around 11:45 p.m., and then returned to the security room around 12:00 a.m. Though he kept an eye on the live camera footage, he admits to falling asleep at some point during his shift, where he stayed asleep until opening at 9:00 a.m. the next morning. He was promptly terminated, but this information would further ignite the public outcry against AMC. You want to avoid admitting this during the negotiation with OMA, though you won't have a choice if they ask directly. It is also true that the sculpture was left unsecured while on display—complete oversight by everyone at AMC.

AMC's executive director has been trying to reach Alexei Martial to question him about his last visit to Propolis. It's no secret that Alexei is obsessed with the statue, and its disappearance the night before Alexei's sabbatical is quite suspicious. He isn't answering the director's calls, and no one is sure where he went. Everyone wants to know if Alexei stole Propolis, but you don't have any more information.

OMA's demand for $17.8 million is completely outrageous. The contract lays out AMC's liability in the event of irreparable damage; nothing in the contract stipulates that AMC would pay for loss of future revenue, loss of invaluable asset, or for the rest of the time Propolis was on loan. You are confident a judge would not rule in favor of OMA to this amount, but it's a delicate situation for you to navigate. The director does not want to offend OMA with a low counteroffer. However, this scandal could seriously decrease AMC's revenue, making it difficult to pay any damages at all. The director believes OMA is entitled only to the $10 million for "irreparable damage" to Propolis provided by the contract. They are willing, however, to show good faith with a $12.5 million offer. In exchange, they want OMA to help repair some of the damage to AMC's reputation. The director has given you authority to decide how to execute this, and has mentioned a public letter of forgiveness as a potential option to try to stop the circulation of the hashtag. OMA is unlikely to agree unless they are satisfied with your financial offer. The director has given you authority to make the final decision in this regard.

In the executive director's attempts to locate Martial, they contacted an artist named Michel Cabern, a relatively obscure sculptor based a few hours south of Argento. He claims to have discovered Pieter Petrov's techniques for creating his ultralight sculpture. The director visited Cabern's studio, and to his delight found a myriad of works, including ten-foot sculptures weighing only a few pounds each.

Cabern agreed to recreate Propolis, subject to OMA's approval. You aren't sure if OMA will be interested in this piece, but if the negotiation goes well, you will offer Cabern's commission. Cabern has also mentioned the many young artists they have trained, each interested in furthering their artistic education. Cabern has nowhere to send them since he remains relatively unknown in the art sphere. He would like help with this in exchange for recreating Propolis. You don't have any ideas right now, but perhaps OMA has a solution. This can help the two museums collaborate and create a good public image while continuing their amicable relationship.

Petrov's other works have caught the attention of the Argento locals and tourists, and you would love for OMA to loan you more works in the future. There is one piece in particular, a painting named *Brood* that AMC's director has instructed you to try to secure for display. They are willing to offer anything that OMA requests in contractual terms but is hoping to pay $80,000 maximum. A new contract will need to be drafted, which you have full authority to create with the other side.

The Latest Buzz
Responding Party Information

Responding Party: OMA

The loss of Propolis has come as a serious blow to OMA. The Ostrovian people are devastated, as are the directors of the museum, who have lost substantial revenue as a result. While it is astounding that this occurred, and everyone involved is seriously upset at AMC, OMA is not ready to sever ties with AMC just yet. Though Petrov's exhibition resulted in an influx of tourism from wealthy art aficionados, few people can afford to visit the remote island of Ostrov. So, while you have high expectations from this negotiation, OMA's director has made it clear that they want to benefit from a potential future relationship.

You must first understand the circumstances of Propolis's disappearance. You've heard rumors that Alexei Martial had become completely obsessed with the sculpture. You also know that he was last seen alone with it just before the museum closed on the night before it's disappearance, which is suspicious. There are rumors floating around Ostrov that a few shards of stained glass were found near the west exit of the museum. If this is true, you would have expected AMC to alert you right away. However, if it is not true, you would be embarrassed to make any harsh accusations and offend AMC. It's best to instead ask many questions about the investigation and determine whether AMC may be hiding something.

You must also ascertain whether AMC took no additional measures to secure Propolis. You feel that from a legal perspective, it is gross negligence not to have done so. If this is so and you litigated, you expect compensation would amount to more than the $10 million for irreparable damages. But the executive director admitted to you in confidence that the initial claim for $17.8 million was made out of anger and they worry that it offended AMC. The director would rather settle for less and continue to benefit from the relationship between OMA and AMC and the connection to Argento. You have been instructed to settle for an absolute minimum of $12.5 million, but more if possible. OMA's director wants the additional $2.5 million to commission a piece to put into the new solarium. They have not yet decided what to display.

Prior to this disaster, one of Petrov's other works from the *Honeybee* exhibit gained popularity on social media. It is a large painting titled *Brood*, an emotionally invoking, abstract piece. OMA was already planning to propose another contract with AMC for the display of this painting as a way to further Petrov's global reputation. Of course, the disappearance has made OMA's executive director extremely apprehensive of this. However, if AMC is agreeable during negotiations, they would accept a new contract which contains security measures and compensation in the event of theft. You have full authority in drafting the contract.

Other museums in Argento are interested in borrowing works from OMA, however they offer substantially less money than AMC. The best offer for *Brood* thus far is from Argenten Contemporary Museum (ACM), which is offering $20,000 to display the piece for one year. OMA will only enter into contracts with ACM if the relationship with AMC dissolves. The director would like $60,000 for a one-year borrow of *Brood.*

As mentioned, the tourism sector did not flourish as much as OMA had hoped or expected following the sudden popularity of Pietre Petrov's works. Flights from the mainland (where Argento is located) to Ostrov are six hours and expensive. OMA is contemplating a program to sponsor art students globally to study under local Ostrov artists, further promoting Ostrov's reputation in the arts. OMA was relying on the further income from Propolis's display at AMC to plan and promote the program; you also need AMC's help to connect you with art students. If the negotiation goes well, you are prepared to put this on the table as a possible future relationship. You will only mention this if you are satisfied with the other conditions of the negotiation.

Tipping the Barrel

General Information

Legendary bull rider Chris Mustang is a fan-favorite rodeo personality. Known for his devil-may-care attitude, he has pulled off some of the most amazing feats ever seen in rodeo history. Mustang is currently under contract with the traveling Rodeo company "Bucking Bronco." Bucking Bronco (BB) travels to fifty cities for fifty weekend-long events throughout the year. While the traveling rodeo is popular for many reasons, its main attraction is undoubtably bull riding. Bull riders are celebrities in the rodeo world and fans attending the events come to cheer on their favorite rider. Ten bull riders compete in every weekend event. The rider who wins each weekend's event (stays on his bull the longest before getting bucked off) is awarded ten points; second place receives six points; third place, four points; two points for the fourth-place finisher; and one point for the fifth-place finisher. The total points for every weekend event are tallied after the fiftieth event to determine Bucking Bronco's "Rider of the Year." The top three finishers contesting for Bucking Bronco's Rider of the Year receive the following cash prizes:

1) First: $150,000
2) Second: $100,000
3) Third: $50,000

Riders finishing in fourth place or below do not receive any prize money.

This year's race for Rider of the Year is tight. Up until last weekend, Chris Mustang was in the lead, being trailed closely by up-and-coming bull rider Hunter Martin. But the weekend did not go as planned for Mustang. Known as the party boy of the bull riding community, Mustang stayed up all night drinking and partying before he was scheduled to compete the following day. He showed up at the rodeo looking visibly intoxicated. The CEO of BB saw Mustang just before he was slated to ride. The CEO told Mustang that he could not in good conscience let an intoxicated rider participate in the rodeo. Mustang argued and the conflict escalated to a profanity-laden shouting match between the pair. Mustang made a rude gesture towards the CEO, and the CEO was overheard saying Mustang would never participate in a BB event again. Not participating in this weekend's event was costly for Mustang. Martin took over as the overall point leader, gaining ten points for a win. Now going into the final weekend of competition, Martin leads Mustang by six points with the third-place contestant a comfortable twenty-two points off the lead.

Tempers subsided after the rodeo was over and Mustang's agent requested the two parties meet at the negotiation/mediation table to hash out their differences. Mustang will be represented by his manager and legal counsel while BB will be represented by its CEO and legal counsel.

Tipping the Barrel
Requesting Party Information

Requesting Party: Mustang's Manager

This is far from the first time Mustang has left himself in a sticky situation. The notorious party animal can be irreverent and sometimes flat-out disrespectful. The CEO was well within his rights to not allow a rider to compete who was intoxicated. But this caused a significant fluctuation in the overall point scale. At today's negotiation/mediation, you are asking for a redo of the competition to give Mustang a chance to regain some much-needed points heading into the final rodeo weekend.

You worry that the CEO might have the ability to fine Mustang for his missed event. Mustang's contract contains a clause stipulating that:

> If a contestant does not compete in an event they are scheduled for due to voluntary intoxication, then that contestant is liable to be fined by the employer up to $10,000 for the infraction at the discretion of the employer.

Worse still, Mustang reportedly yelled, "I'm drunk for half my rodeos!" If this is true, you hope the CEO cannot charge Mustang for being intoxicated at previous events, as this would surely spell financial disaster for Mustang. It could even result in Mustang forfeiting the season. You will do everything you can to avoid discussing Mustang's possible intoxication at previous events.

Mustang entered into his contract with BB without notifying you. In fact, the agreement was made over drinks in the BB head office. You are not particularly tied to Mustang riding exclusively for BB. In fact, you believe the company doesn't take care of its riders. While the payouts for the top three finishers are competitive with other leagues, BB is not a well-respected employer. Riders are prohibited from accepting independent sponsors while riding for BB. You believe a fan favorite like Mustang could make between $20,000–50,000 a year in sponsorship money if they were competing for another organization. Moreover, BB does not sign their athletes to long-term contracts and athletes can be dropped at the end of each season if BB does not want to re-sign them.

One of BB's competitors, Lucky Horseshoe, has approached you and offered Mustang a four-year contract for $100,000 guaranteed per year with the possibility of external sponsors. Mustang still has a year left on his contract with BB, but you believe Lucky Horseshoe would be a much better employer. If you see an opening to leave your contract early with BB you will do so. You know BB's CEO notoriously holds grudges, however, and if he besmudges Mustang's reputation on the free agent market, this could hurt your client's job prospects. Any talk of dissolving Mustang's contract with BB must be approached delicately. You are unsure what Mustang could be entitled to in terms of bonuses as most of these agreements have come through handshake deals. You intend to find out more during this mediation/negotiation.

As Mustang's manager, you know it is all about money for your client. Mustang needs to leave this season with a net $150,000 and has told you if he makes anything less, "you can kiss your job as manager goodbye." Whether Mustang makes this money by winning the season or by alternative means, you need to ensure Mustang leaves the season with a minimum of $150,000 at all costs.

Tipping the Barrel
Responding Party Information

Responding Party: Bucking Bronco CEO

You can't wait to get rid of Mustang and all the organizational headaches he brings with him. You are indifferent on whether Mustang continues to ride with BB and part of you wants to cut ties completely and release Mustang from his contract early (BB owns his rights for one more year). But the reality is that Mustang is one of, if not *the*, *best* riders you have in the rodeo. Not only that, but he is a fan favorite. But up-and-coming rider Martin is poised to boost his name and fan base immensely if he wins this season. You see Martin as the future frontman for BB and will be thrilled if Martin wins this season. Martin is six points on Mustang going into the final rodeo—great for building Martin's brand. You worry, however, that you may have to provide Mustang with a "re-ride" because you shook hands on a deal that stipulated:

> If a rider is deemed ineligible or disqualified from a rodeo, the rider may request a re-ride, where the rider would conduct a private bull ride to see where they would finish within the point standings of that particular rodeo. Upon the completion of the re-ride, if the rider places within the top three in comparison to other riders competing in the rodeo, then the rider would be allocated any points they would have gained as if they had competed in the rodeo. The other rodeo rider's points will also be adjusted accordingly.

Mustang's influence must be considered. Not only is Mustang a fan favorite, but many young riders look up to him. You want to leave this negotiation on good terms with Mustang and his management; Mustang publicly complaining about BB could discourage young bull-riding talent from signing with your organization. Despite his position of influence, you intend to tell Mustang how inappropriate and dangerous it was to show up intoxicated to the rodeo. In fact, you may fine Mustang for his missed event. Mustang's contract contains a clause stipulating that:

> If a contestant does not compete in an event they are scheduled for due to voluntary intoxication, then that contestant is liable to be fined by the employer up to $10,000 for the infraction at the discretion of the employer.

You are uncertain whether to exact a fine. BB is not hurting financially; what you need is a new star bull rider. You would be willing overlook any potential fines provided you do not have to issue a "re-ride."

Moreover, you remember making a separate informal handshake deal with Mustang that if he won fifteen rodeos this year you would pay an additional $50,000 bonus for superior performance. You are unsure that he remembers this conversation as he was quite intoxicated at the time. Mustang has won sixteen rodeos and would be entitled to the $50,000 pay-out you verbally agreed to. BB could be in some hot water if you did not pay this bonus and his management chose to sue. Ideally you won't pay the whole $50,000. You will do your best to avoid bringing up this informal bonus agreement as it could make your organization look unprofessional; however, you are willing to pay Mustang some additional funds (less than $50,000) if the negotiation/mediation goes well.

THE GAMES

General Information

Competing at the Global Sporting Games (the "Games") is a dream shared by many young athletes. Every six years, the world comes together for a celebration of diplomacy and culture through sport at the Games. Ten sporting events are contested in both men's and women's sports, twenty events total over twenty days plus an opening and closing ceremony to crown the best sportspeople and sporting countries on the planet. Simply competing in the Games is a huge feat and is considered a great honor for any athlete talented and fortunate enough to represent their home country. Countries bid more than a decade in advance for the honor of hosting the Games.

Hosting requires significant organization; fifty counties participate in the Games every year. Host countries are required to build or maintain adequate infrastructure to host the many incoming athletes, coaches, staff, and spectators. Significant benefit to the tourism industry can come on the heels of hosting the games, however, making the initial investment in infrastructure worthwhile. This year, the country of Britabella is scheduled to host the Games. For the last ten years, the country has been diligently building stadiums, athlete villages, and roadways, boosting their tourism industry, and more to get ready for the Games. The preparations for the Games seemed to be going without a hitch until recently. . . .

In the last several months the world has been exposed to a new virus, called the X-flu. This newly discovered airborne pathogen is extremely infectious. The virus's effect depends on the individual who has contracted it; while most people recover with little effort, a minority of individuals get seriously ill, and the virus is deadly in a small but significant number of cases. In the past few months, X-flu has spread across the globe. The disease has damaged economies worldwide, and many countries prohibited foreign travelers to enter for fear they carry the virus. Currently, no effective treatment exists to prevent the virus, and patients suffering from X-flu can only have their symptoms treated. People are wary of spreading the virus by close contact and many countries, including Britabella, have mandated mask wearing in congested areas and limited large gatherings in an attempt to slow the spread of the virus.

Despite the introduction of X-flu, the Games are slated to continue as previously scheduled. This didn't sit well with a group of citizens, who organized themselves under the name Britabella Citizens Cooperative (BCC) to advocate for canceling the Games. The group's website notes the increased risk to the health and safety of Britabellans from hosting the Games during the X-flu outbreak. BCC launched a petition that is gaining traction online to cancel the Games. Protests have occurred outside of Britabella government buildings, organized by BCC with chants of "People Before Games" and "No Games in Britabella" echoing through the city.

When questioned publicly about the protests, the Games executives refused to acknowledge BCC and its cause. The executives insist that "those protestors are a radicalized minority" and do not represent the majority of Britabellans. Moreover, the preparations for the Games have already been made (including massive investment in infrastructure). It would be wasteful to undertake all this preparation and not receive the economic boost that inevitably comes from hosting the Games. In contrast, the leaders of BCC have sworn that they will not stop until the Games are cancelled, and they will not hesitate in using "any means necessary" to do so. Things are bound to come to a head soon as the opening ceremony of the Games is only three months away. In a private letter to BCC, the executive committee of the Games requested that representatives of BCC meet at the mediation/negotiation table to voice their concerns. BCC representatives accepted the invitation and posted the invitation to mediation/negotiation letter on their website with the caption "Finally! Some Progress." The Games executive committee will be represented at the table by the president of the executive committee and legal counsel, while the BCC will be represented by their campaign leader and legal counsel.

In the entirety of the discussion about the Games and the impact of X-flu, the government of Britabella has stayed neutral and refused to comment on the conflict when questioned. While they have the final say in whether the Games proceed this year or not, the government has avoided publicly voicing any opinion until negotiations between the Games executives and the BCC are complete.

The Games
Requesting Party Information

Requesting Party: Global Sporting Games Executive Committee

In private meeting, Britabella's president told the executive committee that the Games must go on at all costs. The executive committee and the government of Britabella have taken extensive measures to ensure the Games can happen safely. BCC knows about these measures—they are public knowledge. The health and safety measures already accounted for include:

1) Limiting the venue capacities to maintain "social distancing" requirements;
2) Mandating masks are always worn by coaches and spectators, and by athletes while not competing;
3) Mandating masks in any indoor venues or enclosed spaces and providing an excess of free masks at all the stadiums and the athletes' village;
4) Requiring daily mandatory X-flu testing for all athletes and coaches throughout the competition;
5) Limiting foreign spectators to those holding valid tickets to the Games; and
6) Permitting travel to Britabella only to travelers who test negative for X-flu.

All these precautions have been announced publicly and communicated to all participating athletes and coaches, as well as published on the Games's official webpage. Third-party health and safety organizations suggested these measures and endorsed the above as adequate to ensure the health and safety of everyone involved in the Games. Multiple safety consultants have concurred that if the Games operates with the above regulations, it is unlikely that the concentration of X-flu in Britabella will increase. You intend to make these already-existing health and safety measures clear to BCC, which you feel is portraying your organization unfairly. Moreover, the executive committee was understandably frustrated when BCC published your private letter on their webpage. The president of the executive committee will convey that you believe this was in bad taste and that future publication of private correspondence is unprofessional.

Canceling the games could reflect poorly on the country's leadership and organizational capabilities. But Britabella's government choosing to continue the Games against the wishes of a significant portion of the population would appear totalitarian and could be politically disastrous. As such, the president of Britabella has pledged privately to the executive committee that the country can set aside up to a maximum additional 50 million brits (Britabellan currency) for health and safety mitigations to appease BCC and get them to drop their petition. If 50 million brits is not enough to cover the damage, the Games can contribute 5 million brits of their own funding. If additional funding is required to meet BCC's requests, a new funding solution will be required. The executive committee worries that BCC's activism could extend to visible protesting during the Games. You want BCC to issue a public statement condemning the protests and discouraging BCC supporters from future protests. Ideally, this statement would also emphasize the measures the Games have gone to in promoting health and safety in such turbulent times.

It is important to the executive committee that the collaborative spirit of the Games is reflected at the mediation/negotiation table. The executive committee recognizes that a good relationship with BCC is crucial to the success of the Games.

The Games
Responding Party Information

Responding Party: Britabella Citizens Cooperative

While the BCC movement originally began as an attempt to stop the Games from happening altogether, considering X-flu, it quickly became clear that doing so would prove harder than BCC organizers thought. While stopping the Games entirely may prove difficult, BCC organizers would appear weak if they folded on their demands. Both the Games executives and the Britabella government have refused to acknowledge BCC or make a statement of the group publicly, frustrating the organizers. BCC is willing to be more lenient in negotiations provided their cause is acknowledged and shown adequate respect.

BCC recognizes its mistake in publishing the private correspondence between the Games executives and BCC. This was not meant in poor taste or disrespect to the Games, and such should be emphasized at the table today. Moreover, it would be a shame if pre-existing ill will derailed discussions at the table, as BCC has some important ideas. BCC is aware that the Games will proceed, as the government is unlikely to backtrack on the massive investment it has already made. However, they are concerned with safety and responsibility on the part of the executive committee. BCC is aware that the executive committee's protective measures include:

1) Limiting the venue capacities to maintain "social distancing" requirements;
2) Mandating that masks are always worn by coaches and spectators, and by athletes while not competing;
3) Mandating masks in any indoor venues or enclosed spaces and providing an excess of free masks at all the stadiums and the athletes' village;
4) Requiring daily mandatory X-flu testing for all athletes and coaches throughout the competition;
5) Limiting foreign spectators to those holding valid tickets to the Games; and
6) Permitting travel to Britabella only to travelers who test negative for X-flu.

While third-party evaluators believe these precautions will lower the chances of spreading X-flu, no experts have gone on record saying that rates of X-flu will not go up in Britabella after the Games. In fact, many articles from scientific contributors indicate that the rates of X-flu are bound to increase with more people entering the country for the Games.

Hospitals and medical operations are near capacity in Britabella with just the citizens. BCC worries that with the influx of people the Games and increased concentrations of people will push hospitals to their breaking point and leave Britabellan citizens without adequate medical treatment.

BCC has two additional health and safety measures they wish to propose at the table today:

1) Increased hospital and treatment centers for Britabellan citizens affected by X-flu. This will cost around 50 million brits and will ensure that hospitals will not be overcrowded with X-flu patients if the Games cause a spread of the virus.
2) A Britabella-wide X-flu awareness campaign and mask distribution. This is going to cost around 10 million brits.

BCC is not willing to drop its efforts if these conditions are not incorporated into the Games. BCC is willing and able to help raise the necessary funds to enact these measures and is confident its supporters will donate 3–5 million brits; the rest would need to come from other sources. If the Games executive committee can prove they have adequately accounted for safety precautions for the Games, then BCC will drop the petition. In addition to the previous requests, BCC wants a public statement acknowledging the importance of health and safety in the Games, the measures the organizers will enact to ensure compliance, and BCC's vital role in making the Games safer for everyone. They feel this recognition will put an end to the protests by appeasing the more radical members of their cooperative. Ultimately, BCC recognizes that the two parties at the table today need each other for a successful and safe Games and BCC is willing to cooperate to make this a reality.